Spiritus

Brighter Spheres

Spiritus

Brighter Spheres

ISBN/EAN: 9783337173579

Printed in Europe, USA, Canada, Australia, Japan

Cover: Foto ©ninafisch / pixelio.de

More available books at **www.hansebooks.com**

BRIGHTER SPHERES.

BY

SPIRITUS.

Dictated through the mediumship of

ANNIE F. S.

With an Introduction by E. J. C.

"There is no death ! What seems so is transition.
This life of mortal breath
Is but a suburb of the life elysian,
Whose portal we call death."
              LONGFELLOW.

MONTREAL :
JOHN LOVELL & SON.
1890.

THE AUTHOR'S DECLARATION.

To whom it may concern: I, Spiritus, known throughout this work as Arthur Rogers, do solemnly assert that I dictated it; and that all contained herein is the true account of my life, with its sins, its sorrows, its struggles and final ending.

My object in giving this book to the world is referred to in the beginning of Chapter II.; and again in Chapter XVIII., entitled "My Mission," where, also, is described the process, or agency, employed. Chapter XIX., on "The Use and Abuse of Spiritualism," touches further upon the method of its production.

One thing I would have understood. This book was not written under control, but by direct dictation. The names are assumed, but the characters and scenes are real, the facts true; and to the common Father of all do I dedicate it.

"Not as I will, O Father, but as Thou wilt;" and if it please Thee to let the world reject it, help Thy servants, whose hopes are centred in its success, to commend it to Thy care, and echo with me these words:

"THY WILL BE DONE."

INTRODUCTION.

READER—Believe me or not as you may, this work, which I trust will prove instructive as well as interesting, was produced in the marvellous manner described further on. This is a statement, the truth of which can be supported by many well-known persons, including professional and business men, who were invited on various occasions to witness the progress of the work, and whose names can be furnished should any doubt arise in your mind as to the possibility of this book being the *direct dictation* of an " Invisible Intelligence."

There can be no possibility of imposture on the part of the Medium, who is without the benefits of a liberal education. She is an English-Canadian, educated at the Day schools of Montreal, which she left at the age of fourteen. During the entire progress of the work, she followed her daily avocations away from home; and it was in the evenings that a friend and myself, with others, as already mentioned, witnessed her extraordinary gift of mediumship, which was exhibited in this wise :—She sat by herself at a table with a small empty box thereon, on which she no sooner placed her hands than the said box began to tilt out words and sentences according to the established Spiritualistic Code, which were taken down by one of those present, each tilt representing a letter of the alphabet in its consecutive order—the result being this book.

The Medium is not a "Professional," and never received any pecuniary consideration for the exhibition of her gift, which was witnessed by myself and others under the severest tests. I may add, too, that the sublime soliloquies, and appropriate quotations from poets of past centuries, with which this book is interspersed, clearly prove the utter impossibility, under her surroundings, of fraud on her part, and that the "Invisible Intelligence" dictating the work was outside the Medium; was moreover possessed of considerable ability; and had evidently received a superior education.

And now a few words as to the inception of this book :—The writer of this Introduction has for many years closely studied the theory and philosophy of Spiritualism—or Spiritism, which is the more correct term. He has witnessed, under test conditions, numerous phenomena connected therewith, and has arrived at the conclusion that by a magnetic influence, possessed by certain persons, commonly called Mediums, and under certain conditions, we are enabled to converse with friends and loved ones who have gone before into the unseen world.

It was at a *séance* in the summer of 1889, the unknown but necessary psychological conditions proving favorable, and Annie F. S. being the Medium, that the Author of this book announced his presence under the name of "Friend," and when asked if he had anything to communicate, replied in the following words :—

"I want you to write all I tell you—my life, earthly and immortal. It will be a benefit to all mankind. You will publish it. It will sell well as coming from a higher sphere. Half the profits to go to the poor."

When asked what title the work should bear, the reply came, "Brighter Spheres." He declined to give his own name, but gave that of "Spiritus" as a *nom de plume*. It was then and there arranged when the sittings should take place—which, it may here be stated, occupied a period of about five months.

The reader's attention is especially drawn to the object of the work, as expressed in the opening of the 2nd chapter:—"As thousands of lives are every day filled with darkness and sin, knowing nothing of Eternal Light, it is for them I send forth this work—*a written testimony, a wonderful proof, of glorious immortality;* may it accomplish that mission for which it was destined."

In conclusion, it is hoped no one will be deterred by the words "Medium" and "Spiritism" from reading this book, and that it will be perused in a spirit of fairness and Christian charity, uninfluenced by prejudice or bigotry.

Without delaying the reader any longer from the treat which it is anticipated is awaiting him in the perusal of the following pages, he is requested to read, mark, learn, and inwardly digest the following extracts from two well-known writers on Spiritism, with which the writer of this Introduction bids adieu to the reader:

"He who, in regard to terrestrial magnetism, knows only the little figures of ducks, which with the aid of a magnet are made to swim about in a basin of water, would find it difficult to understand that those toy figures contain the secret of the mechanism of the universe and of the movements of worlds. He whose knowledge of Spiritism is confined to the table turning, which was the starting point of the modern manifestations, is in a similar position ; he regards it merely as an amusement, a social pastime, and cannot understand how a phenomenon so simple and so common, known to antiquity and even to savage tribes, can be connected with the weightiest questions of psychology and of human life. For the superficial observer, what connection can exist between a table that tilts and the morality and future destiny of the human race? But as from the simple pot, which in boiling raises its lid (a pot, too, which has boiled from the remotest antiquity), there has issued the potent motor with whose aid man transports himself through space and suppresses distance, so be it known to you, O ye who know naught of Spiritism, there has issued from the table-tilting, which provokes your disdainful smiles, a new philosophy, that furnishes the solution of problems which no other has been able to solve. I appeal to all honest adversaries of Spiritism, and I adjure them to say whether they have taken the trouble to study what they criticize— reminding them that criticism is necessarily of no value unless the critic knows what he is talking about. Assuredly, if we had presented this philosophy as being the product of a human brain, it would have met with less disdain, and would have had the honor of being examined by those who profess to be the leaders of opinion ; but it claims to be derived from spirits : 'What an absurdity !' exclaim its adversaries. But put aside all thought of the origin of this book ; suppose it to be the work of a man, and say in truth and honesty whether, after having carefully read it, you find in it anything to laugh at or ridicule?

"Strange to say, some of those who are most incredulous in regard to Spiritism deny the possibility of its phenomena in the name of religion, of which they often know as little as they do of Spiritism. They do not reflect that, denying without restriction the possibility of the 'marvellous' and the 'superhuman,' they deny religion, for is not religion founded on revelation and miracles? and what is revelation, if not extra-human communications? All the sacred writers, from Moses downwards, have spoken of this order of communications.

"Spiritism is strong, because its bases are those of religion itself, viz.: God, the soul, the rewards and punishments of the future: because it shows those rewards and punishments to be the *natural* results of the earthly life. In ancient times it was the object of mysterious studies, carefully hidden from the vulgar and illiterate; at the present day it has no secrets, but speaks clearly, without ambiguity, mysticisms or allegories. The time having come for making known the truth, its language is such as all may comprehend; it is not the work of any man; no one can claim to have created it, for it is as old as creation itself; it is to be found everywhere and in all religions.

"'Do Spirits,' it is sometimes asked, 'teach us anything new in the way of morality, anything superior to what has been taught by Christ?' 'If the moral code of Spiritism be no other than that of the Gospel, what is the use of it?' This mode of reasoning is singularly like that of the Caliph of Omar, in speaking of the Library of Alexandria: 'If,' said he, 'it contains only what is found in the Koran, it is useless, and in that case must be burned; if it contains anything that is *not* found in the Koran, it is bad, and in that case also it must be burned.'

"No; the morality of Spiritism is not different from that of Jesus; but we have to ask in our turn, whether before Christ men had not the law given by God to Moses? Is not the doctrine of Christ to be found in the Decalogue? Will it therefore be contended that the moral teaching of Christ is useless? We ask still further of those who deny the utility of Spiritism, why it is that the moral teachings of Christ are so little practised, and why it is that those who rightly proclaim their sublimity are the first to violate the first of His laws, viz: that of 'Universal Charity?'"—*Allan Kardec.*

"Will Spiritism die out? Yes, *if* some dread spell shall change the tides of human life, and turn back their onward flow. Yes, *if* the constitution of human nature can be altered, so that reason and love shall abdicate, and man be something else than man. *If* the law of miracle can be established, *if* caprice can rule the world, Spiritism may die out. *If* the voices of the Immortals can be hushed in eternal silence, or human ears no longer list thereto, or human love respond in harmony to their most kindly greetings, then may, then will it cease to be. When Spiritualism dies, man will die. Philosophy and Science will be buried in the same grave, and the pall of eternal night will fall upon the realm of life. The songs of eternity will cease, its music hushed in eternal silence. All suns will cease to shine, and worlds will wander darkling in the abyss of endless night."—*Professor J. S. Loveland.*

E. J. C.

MONTREAL, March 1890.   134 Peel Street.

CONTENTS.

Chapter I.
A Scene from my Boyhood.................... 9

Chapter II.
New Trials... 15

Chapter III.
Rose... 24

Chapter IV.
A Wealthy Heiress............................... 34

Chapter V.
Prospects of a Wedding....................... 44

Chapter VI.
Married Life... 56

Chapter VII.
The Return of a Lost Love................... 67

Chapter VIII.
Flight.. 77

Chapter IX.
Retribution... 88

CHAPTER X.
My New Friends.................................... 100

CHAPTER XI.
Blighted Hopes.................................... 111

CHAPTER XII.
Parted 126

CHAPTER XIII.
Free at Last...................................... 136

CHAPTER XIV.
The Wages of Sin.................................. 149

CHAPTER XV.
Closing Scenes.................................... 161

CHAPTER XVI.
The Spirit World.................................. 175

CHAPTER XVII.
Scenes I Behold................................... 189

CHAPTER XVIII.
My Mission.. 200

CHAPTER XIX.
The Use and Abuse of Spiritualism................. 209

CHAPTER XX.
The End... 217

BRIGHTER SPHERES.

CHAPTER I.

A SCENE FROM MY BOYHOOD.

Many long years have elapsed and fled—sunk beneath the ocean of time—since my eyes last rested on the scene I am about to describe.

The old house stands there still—now sombre and grand; then it was an ivy-covered homestead.

The day on which my story opens was a hot one in July. High in the heavens the glorious sun was beaming, casting its rays of golden light over all the landscape, and on the running brook till its clear waters sparkled in spontaneous gladness.

In the old-fashioned garden various bright-hued flowers were shedding faint odors on the summer air, and the droning of the busy bee sounded dreamily in the sunshine. Aged trees spread their branches towards the placid sky, while a gentle wind noiselessly stirred their verdant foliage.

Underneath one of those trees a boy is standing. He is only in his fifteenth year, but his well-knit and sturdy frame gives him a look of early manhood, and his dark, lowering countenance and scowling eyes tell of passions pitiful to behold in one so young. He is evidently in a rage. Ever and anon he glances towards a by-path that skirted near the place where he is standing.

Some ten minutes passed slowly by, when another boy came walking along the path. He was some years younger, tall and slightly built, with fair girlish features. He gave a low cry of surprise on seeing the other boy, who bounded forward and stood before him.

"Why, Arthur!" he exclaimed, "what are you doing here? Have you been waiting for me?"

"Yes," replied the other, in a tone of suppressed rage. "I intend to have it out with you. I will teach you to call me a coward and a liar." As he spoke he drew back and struck the other a blow in the face, which was quickly returned; and now the beauty of the scene is gone, for peace has fled, and in its stead there reign high words, angry blows, and cries of rage.

O angel of peace, how often does man insult the presence of thy sanctity! Thou bright messenger of God, descending from regions of untold bliss into the busy haunts of man and sin, and whether to the hovel of the wretched or the lofty ancestral halls of the great, to the cabin of the peasant or the palaces of kings, to the hearts wearied with the world's conflict or the soul battling with despair, thou dost take to them all divine comfort and harmony that tell of the life beyond!

Backward and forward the boys wrestled, the younger getting the worst, for the blood was streaming down his face.

Unperceived by either of them, a lady had appeared on the scene. She was small and delicately formed, bearing the unmistakeable signs of recent illness. Traces of beauty still lingered in her worn countenance. The once sparkling eyes were now dull and sunken, and the luxuriant hair was streaked with silver, showing that time, relentless time, had done its work.

She paused, horror-struck, on seeing the fight. She called aloud to them in an agony of entreaty. She asked them in imploring accents to stop; yet they heeded her not—did not seem to hear her.

But it was now over. One well-directed blow, which took the younger off his feet, sent him heavily to the earth, his head coming in contact with a large rock. He lay motionless, white and still.

A sharp cry of intense agony from the woman caused the victor to turn in her direction. A deathlike pallor had overspread her features. One hand was clasped convulsively over her heart. She was gasping as if for breath. "Murderer!" she cried, gazing at him with reproachful eyes. Then in milder accents she murmured, "O God, have mercy on my boy!" A shuddering of the body, a contraction of the features, a low moan, and all was still; the sorrow and pain were all ended, for she was dead, and nothing remained but the pale, silent body to mock my anguish, for I, Arthur Rogers, was that boy, and the woman, lying dead and cold beside me, was my mother.

With breathless haste I hurried to the house, which was quite near, to summon aid. My father was away from home, but a Miss Waters, who was staying at the house, ran, with the frightened servant, to the spot. The boy, who was merely stunned, was sent for the nearest doctor, while I helped to carry the lifeless body of my mother, which we laid gently on her bed; and I bent over her, in vain endeavoring to restore life to her inanimate form, for I could not believe that she was dead. For years she had been suffering from heart-disease, and, the week before, her physician had told us that the least shock or excitement would prove fatal. Arriving at the scene when she did, and witnessing the fall of my comrade, she thought I had killed him. The thought of her boy a murderer was more than the weak heart could bear.

The doctor soon arrived and told us, after a brief examination, that it was only what he expected; and hurried away to his other patients. Miss Waters went to telegraph for my father, who was in New York; and I was alone with the dead, filled with remorse for the past and fear for the future. How well I knew that I had caused her death, and that through life I had been her greatest care. How often had I brought tears of sorrow to the dear eyes now closed in death; and those lips, that had that morning kissed me, were now sealed for eternity, and the familiar voice was hushed for ever—for I knew not that her spirit still watched over her boy.

O ye Christians, how blessed is the knowledge that enables you to think of your loved ones as not dead, but gone before, where, in some higher, brighter sphere, they wait for you to join them!

But I knew nothing of this. To me the future held no hope, no great hereafter. How often, in the dreary nights that followed, would I wake from some troubled dream, and fancy that she stood beside me, her hand laid on my burning head, while in the darkness the night-wind seemed to waft her dying words through my frenzied brain, "O God, have mercy on my boy!"

CHAPTER II.

NEW TRIALS.

BEFORE passing over the few years that separated my boyhood from manhood, I would like to give the reader an insight into my character, in order that he may judge whether the evil that surrounded my life was the result of my early training, or that criminal inheritance, or natural tendency to sin, so characteristic of man. I would like to portray my life as it really was. As thousands of lives are every day filled with darkness and sin, knowing nothing of eternal light, it is for them I send forth this work—a written testimony—a wonderful proof of glorious immortality. May it accomplish that mission for which it was destined!

Mine was a disposition that loved freedom; and I longed for the time when I could throw all control aside and be my own master. Possessed of a violent, hasty temper, I was often led into acts of cruelty and injustice. My father, who was an atheist, had early instilled into my mind lessons unnatural to youth and opposed to Christianity. He was a hard, stern man, believing in neither God nor Devil, and was greatly feared by all the household. He was successful in business as a New York merchant, but had retired from it on his marriage with my mother.

She was an English lady of good birth, a sincere Christian, and of a timid, clinging nature, easily governed by a man like my father.

When I was very young, she began to teach me baby prayers and Bible verses. My father, entering unexpectedly one day, and hearing me repeating what I had learned, flew into a rage, and I never forgot the scene that followed; it made an impression on my childish mind. He swore that he was not going to have my head filled with such nonsense; it was only fit for smooth-faced parsons. In vain my mother pleaded that there was some truth in religion, and that a God really existed; he would not listen; he said it was all superstition, and that if she did not stop teaching me such trash, he would send me away where I would learn something sensible.

This was sufficient to frighten her into giving

the required promise; but it was a heavy blow to her, and, like some pale, delicate flower, she began to fade and droop in the cold atmosphere of our uncongenial home.

Some years after this, when I was old enough to begin my education, my father sent me to one of his friends in Boston—an atheist like himself—where a tutor of the same sect was engaged for me, and I began my studies away from a mother who alone understood the failings of her boy. Among other things I was taught that religion was false, and, as it had originated in the dark ages, like all superstitions it would soon die out. Thus I became an unbeliever.

All this helped to break my mother's heart. Growing to manhood apart from her tender care, her's was the earnest prayer that daily rose beyond the eternal heaven in my behalf—prayers that were not answered till she had slept long years in her peaceful grave.

With her death new trials awaited me. It was the day after she died, and I was sitting alone in the long dining-room, anxiously waiting my father's arrival. It was a bright day, full of gladness. Outside the birds sang gaily, and all nature seemed rejoicing, contrasting deeply with the gloom and solitude within. The radiant sunshine strayed through the curtained window and rested in patches of rosy light on the carpet, and one gentle ray lingered lovingly on my solitary figure, as if pitying me in my loneliness.

Those who have experienced a boyish grief must know how fleeting it is. My first burst over, I longed to throw off the impression of gloom, and, in the open air, revel in some boyish sport, that I might forget my sorrow. Here everything reminded me of my loss: on the table the work-basket, with its dainty needlework, and the book she had been reading; and on the floor her pet dog, lying waiting for the well-known footsteps that he would never hear again.

The quiet stillness of the room began to oppress me, and I fell into a train of gloomy thought. I wondered how my father would bear the news of my mother's death. Would he sink beneath a storm of grief? or fly into a rage with me as being the indirect cause of her death? or would he bear it with that stolid indifference which I knew was part of his nature?

My reverie was interrupted by the opening

and the closing of the door, and, turning round, I saw that Miss Waters had entered. As she is to figure in these pages, I owe her a brief description. To begin with, she had taken a great dislike to me, which I heartily returned. She was a haughty-looking creature above the average height, with dark swarthy countenance, and features that, in spite of their haughty repose, were rather handsome. Her chief attraction, however, lay in the expression of the dark, flashing eyes. She was magnificently attired in some bright color that seemed out of place in a house of mourning. She swept languidly across the floor, giving the unoffending dog a savage kick.

"You leave that dog alone," I cried out sharply, but she took no notice of me; only a slight flush of anger overspread her face, which plainly showed that she was annoyed.

She seated herself in an easy chair near the window and drew back the curtain.

"I wonder what time your father will arrive," she asked, after a short silence; "I hope he will come soon, for this house needs a master. That poor, weak creature, your mother, was utterly incapable of managing a household. Things are all upside down."

My temper was rising, for I knew that she lied. My mother was a model housekeeper. I made no reply but gave the speaker a look of withering contempt. She was, however, determined to aggravate me. Taking up a book off the table, she began hurriedly to turn over the pages. Now it happened to be my mother's Bible.

"Silly thing," she said, with a sneer, "how could she believe all this stuff? I pity your father. He must have been unhappy, tied to a religious maniac who thought more of religion than of him."

"You lie," I shouted, springing to my feet in anger, for the slighting way in which she spoke of my mother maddened me.

"You are an insolent wretch," she hissed, " to speak to a lady in that manner."

"A lady!" I retorted, scornfully. "Do you act the part of a lady, sneaking around the house, fighting with the hired girl, prying into domestic affairs, and insulting the memory of her whom you called friend? and understand," I added, "that, until my father's arrival, I am master here."

Not trusting myself to say any more, I hurried

from the room, followed by the frightened dog, and the low, mocking laugh of my adversary reached me as I closed the door. I felt as if I hated her, and would gladly have crushed her out of my life.

"Who is she?" I asked myself. "What gives her so much authority?"

I had once heard that her family and my father's were intimate for years. "But," I thought, angrily, "that is no reason why she should 'boss' the whole house."

I spent the remainder of the day in my room, and had serious thoughts of running away. I thought if I could go far away, I would win fame and wealth, for never did human heart pant more ardently than mine to be distinguished. But alas for the dreams of youth, never to be realized!

I had just finished counting over my small stock of money, when some one entered the room, and, looking up, I was face to face with my father. One glance at his stern countenance told me that I need not expect any pity from him. If any grief had pressed his heart, it had left no visible sign. There was no trace of sorrow in that set, determined face.

"Well," he said, sternly, "what have you to say about all you have done?"

I was beginning to explain the circumstances of my mother's death, but he interrupted me with an impatient gesture.

"Spare me all explanations," he cried, "Miss Waters has told me all; and, not content with being the cause of a serious accident, you have deliberately insulted a lady for whom I have a sincere regard."

"It seems so," I replied, "since you think more of what you call an insult than you do of the death of your wife."

"Silence!" he shouted, "do not answer me in that voice. You must apologize to the lady."

"Never," I answered. "I did only what I would do again were she to speak lightly of my mother."

He gave me an angry look. "Do you know, sir," he said, "that I am going away for some time, and have made arrangements for you to live under this lady's care during my absence?"

"Live under her care!" I repeated; "no, I will leave the house first."

"As you will," he replied, indifferently. "You can go to your aunt in New York and finish your education. Miss Waters will remain here and look after the house."

"All right," I replied, calmly, though my heart seemed bursting.

He turned to leave the room. "You will be ready by the last of the week," he said. Then without another word he left me.

On the impulse of the moment, I would have run after him and asked for a little sympathy, a little love; but, on second reflection, I knew how useless it would be, and I returned to my solitary thoughts, all hopes of escape banished, for I felt that he would watch me.

During the years that followed, in which I grew to manhood, I often thought that my father had spoiled my whole life. But I was in the hands of a higher power than his—yet I knew it not—a Power that was gradually leading me on till that time when all things would be right and I should know the truth.

CHAPTER III.

ROSE.

It is a dull winter's evening in the city of New York. A light snowstorm is rising, filling the air with tiny flakes that flutter against the window-panes, as if anxious to get in, and then fall softly to the ground where they are soon trodden out of sight by the passers-by.

In the interior of a large, well-furnished room, two persons are seated. The elder, a tall, dark young man, slightly bronzed, is myself grown to manhood. My companion is a lady, young and beautiful. She is a brunette, with a clear, olive complexion just tinted with a soft bloom. Her features are small and regular. The eyes, dark and liquid, are now filled with a bewitching light; and the shapely head is surmounted by a mass of dark, wavy hair. She is dressed in the height of fashion, in some rich material that fits her well-formed figure to perfection. Costly diamonds flash from the rings on her fingers and gleam in the dusky hair. There is a babyish pout on the pretty features, that reminds me of a spoilt child, and one tiny foot impatiently taps the carpet.

"It is too bad," she exclaimed, "that I cannot go to the ball. You are so unreasonably jealous."

"You are wrong," I said, hotly. "I did not speak without good reason. Have I not been patient, lingering by your side night after night, without a word, a smile, a glance? and while others revelled in the enjoyment of your company, you simply ignored my presence. We had better part," I added moodily. "My love and devotion count as nothing. You no longer care for me."

A momentary look of fear crossed her features, which was replaced by a pleading smile as she rose and came softly towards me.

"You tiresome boy," she said, in a light tone, "can you not see that I do not mean it? that though I amuse myself with others, it is you I really love?"

"You only say that to please me," I answered. "If you loved me, you would act differently."

She made no reply, but gave me a tender

glance from the liquid eyes that caused my anger to melt.

"Why do you torment me so?" I asked. "You seem to take a delight in making me jealous."

"I must live," she cried, with a tragic gesture. "Life would be very dull without a little admiration, a little excitement. But this evening I will devote myself to you. Now, let us be friends."

"My own darling," I cried, with rapture; and then followed a scene which all lovers are familiar with. An hour later, when I said good-bye, I had promised to escort her to the ball; and I walked home with a heart very light indeed, for I believed myself desperately in love. It was that love which most men experience in a lifetime, and which they look back upon in after years with about as much emotion as they would on some childish toy.

Eight years had passed since my mother's death—years during which I studied a little, travelled a little, and grew a little more wicked. I had now entered my twenty-third year, and the world seemed very bright to me. I had not a care nor a thought for the future. My father I seldom saw. He had married Miss Waters; and, as that amiable lady and I were not on very good terms, we saw very little of each other.

They still occupied the old house in the outskirts of Boston, and I lived in New York with my aunt, Mrs. Rogers. She was a good-natured old lady, and, having no children of her own, I was over-indulged by her, so that I did just what I liked. Her husband, who was my father's brother and very much resembled him, I stood a little in awe of, but not enough to prevent me from often staggering home under the influence of too much wine. I had a large income from my father, but I managed to spend it all, and was frequently in debt. I was a well-known sport and gambler, a fair hand at billiards, and the associate of some of the most questionable characters in town; yet in spite of this I had the *entrée* into good society, and was petted by numerous mammas with marriageable daughters. I had, however, already found my ideal, not in some well-known heiress or fashionable belle, but in the person of a poor actress, Rose Ashton, who had nothing save her pretty face and ready wit to recommend her. I have already described her to the reader in the beginning of the chapter. To me she was the impersonation of all womanly grace and beauty. I had known her about three months.

The first time I had seen her was on the stage. I had sauntered into the theatre with some of my friends to see the play. It was badly produced, but the acting was good, and my fancy was attracted by the face and figure of the leading star. Hearing that one of my companions knew her, I sought an introduction, which was granted, and I soon joined the host of numerous admirers that nightly thronged around her, and vied with each other in showering costly gifts on the object of their devotion. At first I was the favorite. I bought the rarest jewels, and "stood" the most expensive suppers. Sometimes a richer rival would appear on the scene; then I was slighted and thrown aside. I soon let her know that I was not going to stand this; and we had many an angry scene, which always ended in a compromise from her and some costly presents from me. News of all this soon reached my father's ears, and he threatened to stop my allowance, but had not done so yet.

The night of the ball arrived. It was a clear night, with just a suspicion of frost in the December air. Rose was in a flutter of excitement. She was looking very lovely in a dress of soft white silk, relieved by clusters of crimson roses.

> " O woman ! lovely woman ! nature made thee
> To temper man ; we had been brutes without you." *

We were late entering the ball room. Dancing had commenced, and many admiring glances followed Rose, who was undoubtedly the belle. The scene was lovely to gaze upon. I often recalled it in after years—the long, brilliantly-lighted room with its highly polished floor—the lofty ceiling almost hidden beneath a profusion of flowers and rare tropical plants, arranged with exquisite taste.

The pleasures of life are very short! Alas, all earthly joys are fleeting! Sometimes we try to seize them, but they elude our grasp and float away from us for ever.

That night, or rather early the next morning, when I returned home, I was surprised to find my aunt sitting up for me—a thing I had never known her to do before.

---

*Otway, Venice Preserved.

"What is wrong?" I asked breathlessly, as she beckoned me into the library.

"Your father!" she exclaimed, in agitation. "He has arrived, and is in an awful rage. He has heard something about you."

"About me!" I echoed. "What can he mean?"

"I don't know," she replied. "He accused me of letting you go to ruin."

"Never mind," I said, soothingly. "You are not to blame, I will make it all right."

"You don't know what a rage he is in," she rejoined.

"I don't care," I said, angrily. "I will let him see that it is no boy he has to deal with. I am now a man, and can judge for myself."

I soon retired, but not to rest. I had a troubled dream in which I beheld Rose pursued by a demon who had the face of my father, and I awoke filled with gloomy forebodings. The first thing after breakfast he sent for me, and we had a stormy scene. I was steadfast, and vowed never to part from Rose, and that I intended to marry her as soon as her engagement at the theatre was ended.

"You will do no such thing," my father

roared, as he angrily paced the floor. "If you disgrace yourself by wedding that creature I will disown you. You talk about love, but this is only a boyish fancy. Return home with me and you will soon forget it."

"It is no boyish fancy," I retorted. "I never will forget her."

"'When poverty enters the door, love flies out at the window,'" he quoted.

I was too angry to make any reply. I felt that I must see Rose and tell her all that had passed; so I seized my hat and hurried from the house.

"She will be true," I murmured to myself. "Poverty will not change her love."

I found her looking a little pale and tired from the effects of the night before. She looked surprised to see me at such an early hour. I told her all my father had said.

"You see," I added, "that he wants to part us, but I will never give you up."

"You are wrong," she said, with an angry frown, "I could not live in poverty. You should not have quarreled with your father."

"What!" I cried, in astonishment, "do you know what that would mean? It would be separation from you, misery for us both."

"And what will be the result if you defy him?" she asked. "If you could only exercise a little common sense, you would see that if you give in to him now it will be the better for us. Return home for a while, and, when he sees that you are steadfast, he will soon give in."

"You never loved me," I said, dejectedly, "or you would not send me from you."

"It is because I do love you," she rejoined, "that I do not want to ruin your future. You would be helpless without money."

"Could I not work as other men do?" I said gloomily.

She gave an incredulous smile. "What could you do? You would soon tire; and I want wealth and position. I do not intend to be an actress always," she said, musingly. "I always understood you would be wealthy."

"But," I pleaded, "it is not my fault. If I go from you, how am I to live? life will be so dull."

"Don't talk such nonsense," she said sharply. "There is no alternative; I have made up my mind never to marry a poor man."

I pleaded with her, reasoned with her, but it was all in vain; so we parted, with many assurances of faithful love, and promises to write often.

I was greatly disappointed in Rose, and the cool way she regarded the matter. I had always thought of her as something above the common, but found that she was only a weak, fickle woman. I told my father that I would return home with him for a while; and he, apparently content, made no remark. I left New York with a sad heart, for I felt as if Rose was lost to me forever.

During the journey my father told me that he expected me to marry for position. "With your prospects you ought to make a brilliant marriage," he said. I listened quietly, secretly determined to marry no other woman but Rose.

CHAPTER IV.

A WEALTHY HEIRESS.

I FOUND the old house greatly changed by modern improvements and new faces. I had loved the old-fashioned things of my childhood, but the new Mrs. Rogers followed the latest styles.

It was late when we arrived, and the house was full of company. I made a hasty toilet and descended to the drawing-room, resolved to be as disagreeable as I could. My amiable step-mother came forward and greeted me with great cordiality. She seemed determined to ignore the past, and I thought it was best to fall in with her mood.

"Why, how you have grown!" she exclaimed. "I would not have recognized you. I must introduce you to my niece. Come here, Maud," she cried, "this is Arthur, whom I have already told you about." There was a slight movement in the back-ground as Maud came forward —a girlish figure in simple white—and acknowledged my formal bow.

I was mentally contrasting her pale, subdued beauty, with the rich, glowing loveliness of my first love. Mrs. Rogers left us together, and her niece opened the conversation by asking me some questions about New York society, to which I briefly replied, and led her on to speak of herself. I found she was the only child of Richard Waters—a wealthy Chicago citizen. Her mother had been dead some years, and Mrs. Rogers had kindly offered to chaperon her in society. She then amused me with anecdotes of the neighborhood. She was an agreeable conversationalist, and gifted with a rare sense of humor; and before the evening was over, I was laughing heartily at her sharp wit and merry ways. I asked for music, and listened entranced while she played the pieces I liked best and sang my favorite songs. I grew interested in her, and was ready to declare her a very nice young lady; and my father looked silently on, evidently well pleased that I was, unconsciously, walking into the trap that was set for me.

During the evening my step-mother brought in her two children—two fine, sturdy boys— and I fancied that she gave me a malicious glance as I watched them playing around their father's knee. "This is the reason," I thought bitterly, "why he is so anxious for me to marry well. He wishes to share his own wealth with those boys; and I, his first-born, would be defrauded of my rights!"

The next morning I rose early and sauntered around the old place, recalling scenes of my boyhood. I then wrote a long letter to Rose, in which I assured her of my faithful love, and promised never to forget her.

In the anxious days that followed I waited in vain for an answer. None came. I wrote again and again with the same result. "She has forgotten me," I thought, bitterly; "some wealthier rival has taken my place." Yet I loved her, blindly, madly; and, in spite of her seeming indifference, she was ever in my thoughts. I wrote to the manager of the theatre in which she played, and in a few days received an answer that dashed all my hopes away. She had left the city, and he could obtain no clue to her whereabouts. I now believed her false to me, and, in a fit of jealous rage, devoted myself more than ever to the fair Maud. I was constantly at her side, and Mrs. Rogers took great trouble to throw us in each other's society. She was always planning some party, or driving expedition, which kept us in a whirl of social life; and as the days passed quickly by, I was surprised to find how well I was enjoying myself.

One dull, wet morning in the month of February we were all seated around the breakfast table, merrily laughing and talking, when a telegram was handed to Maud. Her face became deathly in its pallor, and she turned to her aunt with a low cry.

"What is wrong?" we all asked, breathlessly.

"My father!" she sobbed. "He is dying! Oh, I must go to him!"

"You will have to wait," my father said, consulting his watch. "There is no train for two hours. Arthur will go with you; and if anything happens you can return with him."

"Oh, no," she cried, turning to me with a faint blush. "I could not think of troubling Mr. Rogers."

"It is no trouble," I replied. "If you will accept me as your escort I shall deem it an honor."

She thanked me with a sad smile, and in a few hours we started on our journey.

It took me all my time and attention to cheer the drooping spirits of my fair companion. We found the old gentleman sinking fast; the doctor gave no hopes. Indeed he seemed only to be living till his daughter's arrival. I was an unwilling witness to a sad scene that followed, for Maud insisted on my entering the room with her. I saw, in the subdued light of the sick-room, a feeble sufferer with hollow cheeks and staring eyes, which plainly told that death had marked him as a victim. Maud knelt quietly by the bedside—a gentle figure, half child, half-woman. "Father," she said, brokenly "I am here."

"My poor child," he said, faintly. "What is to become of you when I am gone?"

"Don't," she pleaded. "Don't think of it."

"But I must," he said, feebly. "Alone in this desolate world, young and wealthy. Who is that there?" he added, turning towards me.

"It is a friend," Maud replied. "Young Mr. Rogers; he has been very kind to me."

"Come here," the dying man said to me; "draw closer that I may see your face."

I did so, and seemed to feel the searching gaze of his sharp eyes.

"I knew you as a boy," he went on in the same feeble voice, "and you have greatly changed. You are the only one near me whom I can trust. Will you grant a favor to a dying man?'

"What is it?" I asked, bending over him, while Maud gave me a grateful glance.

"My child!" he answered. "I have a strange presentiment that sorrow will overshadow her young life. I have guarded her jealously from all care. Will you promise me, if she ever needs a friend, to help her?"

"Gladly," I answered. "She shall never need a friend while I live."

"Thank you," he murmured; "your father is to be her sole guardian, and may God deal with you as you deal with her." His voice seemed to die away, and he sank into a deep slumber.

I made Maud lie down, promising to call her if there was any change.

All through the dreary night I kept silent watch. Once my eyelids closed and I must have slept, for at daybreak I awoke with a start, and glanced anxiously towards the bed. All was still, and, going near, I perceived that death had silently entered and seized its prey. I roused

Maud and told her. She bore it calmly, standing mute in her sorrow, contemplating the loved features, so awful in their last repose.

"I cannot realize it," she said to me in a whisper. "Is he really dead? and am I alone in the pitiless world?"

"Not alone," I said, gently; "you forget your aunt, my father, and last, but not least, myself."

"That is so different," she replied. "Have you never known a longing to be loved, to be necessary to someone's happiness, or to have some strong heart to lean upon, someone to think for you, someone to love you? Perhaps men are different," she went on; "perhaps you do not mind, as women do. Life seems so empty to look forward to—no mother's love, no father's care, not even a gentle sister or manly brother; I am alone, so utterly alone."

I knew not how to comfort her, yet I felt my heart drawn to her in her loneliness. For the moment Rose was forgotten, as I bent softly over my fair companion and whispered gently: "Let me have a right to protect you from those gloomy thoughts. Try and forget that you are alone in the world; for remember, I promised your father to take care of you."

"You are very kind," she murmured. "I have been thinking so much, my head aches. Death is so awful, so mysterious; the grave, so cold and silent. What is it, I wonder, that lies beyond? Is he dead forever? Is he merely nothing? or do you believe in another life in which he still exists?"

Some lines I had read, written by Blair, flashed through my brain involuntarily—

> "Tell us, ye dead! Will none of you, in pity
> To those you left behind, disclose the secret?
> O! that some courteous ghost would blab it out,
> What 'tis you are, and we must shortly be!
>
> . . . .
> . . . Well—'tis no matter;
> A very little time will clear up all,
> And make us learned as you are, and as close." *

"No," I said aloud, "there is no other life. I cannot believe in a future state. But do not dwell on such things. We know that he is free from suffering."

She gave a low shudder—"I don't like to think of him as dead forever. He was so good—my poor father—and he believed in another existence. I like to picture him in the enjoyment of it. And," she went on, in a plaintive voice, "I was not brought up like other children. I never

---

* Blair—The Grave.

had a loving voice to speak to me of God and heaven."

"Don't talk like that," I said, sharply; "there is nothing in all that nonsense. Religion has no foundation. Come downstairs, away from this chamber of death, and you will feel better."

"Oh, no," she replied, "I must stay with him. I feel as if he knew that I was here. Something seems to whisper in my heart that he still exists. It is the first time that I have come in contact with death, and it oppresses me. Can you not feel its mysterious power?"

"It is natural," I replied; "everyone must die; it is the end of all mankind. To the young and happy it is full of terror, and I think it would be a tyrant to the rich and self-indulgent; but to the wretched and poor it has no terror."

"I know that," she answered, "for it brings them peace. But what comes afterwards? Can you tell me?"

"Nothing," I replied. "Have I not already told you my belief? There is no other life: there is no God."

"Go," she cried, turning from me, "I would rather be alone, as I must henceforth be in life, with none to pity me, none to comfort me."

I saw that she was growing hysterical, and I went downstairs and sought the house-keeper —a kind, motherly soul—and sent her up with some refreshment. She returned in a short time and told me that she had " coaxed Miss Maud to her room," and that her sorrow had been forgotten in a refreshing slumber.

The next few days I was kept very busy, as I had to make all arrangements for the funeral. The day after it took place I advertised the house to let, and returned home, accompanied by Maud—a sad little figure in sombre garments. Yet sorrow had added to her beauty, and given her pensive loveliness that was pleasing to the eye and when at times the image of Rose came before me, I would contrast her as some glowing flower, of which her name was a type, with Maud, who reminded me of a pale, drooping lily.

CHAPTER V.

PROSPECTS OF A WEDDING.

THE long winter months passed away into spring, and I now began to tire of the life I was leading at home, and thought with regret of the gay time I had had in New York. I longed for the excitement of the gaming table, the social dinners at the club, the brilliant receptions in society, and all that had made life a pleasure. My stepmother, too, had cast aside her mask. All the amiable smiles that had at first greeted me were gone, and she was once more the tyrant I had always known her. She sought many ways to annoy me, and was the cause of many quarrels between me and my father, who seemed to think her the model of all things good.

One stormy, wet afternoon, I made up my mind to return to New York. I was in a fit of angry impatience, and sought my father in the library. He was writing at his desk, and his wife sat reading near the window. They both gave me a look of surprise, as I announced my intention of returning to New York.

"Please yourself," my father said coldly, "but what of Maud?"

"Maud!" I echoed blankly. "Why, what has she got to do with it?"

"You act the innocent part well," sneered Mrs. Rogers.

"I don't know what you mean," I retorted sharply.

"Then you must be a bigger scamp than I took you for," she answered, "and quite devoid of all honor."

"Do you think," my father went on in the same cold tone, "that, after striving to gain a woman's love and affection, you can throw it aside like a worthless weed? I am surprised at you."

"But," I said hotly, "I have never thought of such a thing. You know well my heart was given to another before I ever saw Maud, and I only regard her as a friend, or sister."

Mrs. Rogers gave vent to a low scornful laugh. "Does a man loiter in the moonlight, whispering sweet nothings to *his sister*, seeking her company at all times, and paying every lover-like attention to her?" she asked, mockingly.

I gave her a quiet look of contempt, and turned to my father. "Why don't you speak out," I said, "and tell me at once that you wish me to marry Maud because she is rich?"

"Well," he said, uneasily, "you have made it an understood thing; it is your own fault; the whole neighborhood looks upon you as engaged, and you are in duty bound to marry this girl; or, he added, you are no son of mine."

"But Maud herself," I protested; "she may object. I don't see what happiness can result from such a marriage. I have been blind not to foresee this. I suppose it was all your scheme," I added, confronting Mrs. Rogers.

"Indeed!" she sneered, "how ungrateful you are. One would think you were asked to commit some crime, instead of marrying a young and pretty girl."

"I wish I had never come here," I said fiercely. "If I had only remained in New York, I might have been happily married to Rose."

Mrs. Rogers gave an affected laugh. "What a pity!" she said, in a sarcastic voice; "it is too bad that you missed such an honor. Fancy introducing that creature—that play-actress—to me, as your wife."

"Indeed," I replied, with a sneer, "were she my wife, I would not care to introduce her to you."

"Enough of this," my father interposed. "Arthur, you forget yourself. My dear," he added, turning to his wife, " will you kindly leave us?"

"Don't mind that boy," she said, rising and moving languidly across the room, "I never expect anything better from him. I only pity Maud, if she marries him." With this parting thrust, she left the room.

"So," I exclaimed, angrily, to my father, "you and your wife have decided my fate. I am to have no voice in the matter—to have no judgment of my own."

"You are unreasonable," my father replied. "Can you not see that it is all for your good? You will have a good, sensible wife, besides gaining a small fortune. You cannot expect me always to provide you with money. At my death you will have very little, as I have my wife and children to look after."

"I know that," I replied, moodily; "they are

your first thought; it makes no difference whether I am happy or not."

"You are talking nonsense," he retorted; "you will have everything to make you happy; it is your own fault if you are not so. But think the matter over, there is no hurry."

And think it over I did, in the quiet solitude of the night. It was not the prospect of marrying Maud that angered me, so much as not having my own way. No doubt if they had wanted me to marry some one else, I should then have desired Maud in preference to any other woman. "After all," I thought, "she may refuse me. She is a girl of sense, and can see for herself that I have very little love to offer her." But did I love her? that was the question I asked myself, over and over. No, I felt quite sure that I could admire, pity her, but could not love her as she deserved to be loved, for I knew that she was a good woman, and I felt myself unworthy of her.

The next day I took a better view of the matter. It was a hot, sultry Sunday, a day that sometimes comes to us in spring-time, when the sun shines as hot, and the birds sing as gaily, as in midsummer.

I spent the day in my own room trying to make up my mind. "Many a man might do worse," I thought; "she is pretty, graceful, and wealthy. Perhaps it would be the best thing I could do to marry her, if she is willing. Rose is lost to me," I thought bitterly, "and is, no doubt, happy with some other man. Why should I not be happy also?"

Towards evening my spirits rose, showing the fickle nature I possessed, and I determined to speak to Maud at once.

Knowing that she often spent Sunday evenings in the garden, which was one of her favorite haunts, I went out to enjoy my cigar, in the hope of meeting her and hearing her answer to my proposal.

It was a lovely, balmy evening. A soft shower had just fallen, which had refreshed the parched earth, and cooled the atmosphere, making it a pleasure to inhale the fragrant air. Across the meadows came the faint ringing of distant bells. Overhead a silvery moon kept silent watch over the peaceful scene, and I began to wonder, in an uncertain way, if it could but speak, what wonders it might relate, what secrets it might reveal.

The calm, peaceful serenity of the hour seemed to impress me with a sense of unworthiness, and some new-born power seemed to rise within me—a something which I could not define. Perhaps it was the mysterious voice of nature, which sometimes appeals to man; or was it a gleam of divinity, held out to mock my darkened soul, and then withdrawn? for the hour was not yet come—the hour when all darkness would pass away, and my wondering soul behold the eternal light.

A slight noise behind me attracted my attention. It broke the spell; the delight of the moment was gone. I turned round, and mechanically retraced my steps to the spot from whence the sound came, for it sounded like some one in distress. I pulled aside some bushes that overhung a garden chair, and perceived the outline of a woman's figure. "Is anything wrong?" I asked. "Who are you?" At the sound of my voice the figure rose to a standing position, and with surprise I beheld, in the set full moonlight, the features of Maud.

"Speak," I cried, "and tell me what is wrong; has anything happened?"

"You!" she cried, "how dare you speak to

me?" and I felt, rather than saw, the anger and contempt depicted on her countenance. "Is it not enough," she went on, "that you have caused me such misery?"

"What do you mean?" I said, in a tone of surprise; "how am I the cause of your sorrow?"

"My aunt has told me all," she said, brokenly; she has accused me of striving to win your love, and vainly encouraging your attention; and that I, having lost all maidenly reserve, have given you my affection unasked."

"She is a demon!" I interrupted.

"Oh! it is unbearable," she went on, "and unjust. I thought you all that was good and noble, and almost unconsciously my heart found in you a hero. Now," she added, "it is all ended; leave me, well satisfied with the misery you have caused."

"No," I said sternly, "not till you have heard what I have to say. Your aunt has told you her story, no doubt with exaggeration. I said things yesterday, in my anger, that were not meant to be repeated. I know not what you think, or what you have heard; but I do know that this evening I came out here to look for you with the purpose of asking you to be my wife."

She gazed at me for an instant in silent doubt. "You are jesting," she stammered.

"No," I answered, as calmly as I could, "I am in downright earnest; I here ask you, solemnly, to be my wife."

"Oh!' she exclaimed, "what am I to believe? Your manner speaks the truth; if I have wronged you, I am sorry."

"Don't think of that," I said cheerfully; "but I am waiting for an answer to my question."

"Not now," she said, hurriedly. "I must have time; I want to think. Are you quite sure you did not speak through pity?"

"Quite sure," I answered, smiling, "but think it over and let your own heart decide. This day week I will be here in this spot, at this hour, and then you can give me your answer, which I trust will be a favorable one. We can be quietly married and go away to some far distant land, where we will forget all this unpleasantness, all this sorrow."

"I would like that," she said, eagerly, "for I could not live with my aunt any longer. I am so sorry that I have misjudged you."

"Forget it all," I said, "and do not let your aunt influence you in this matter. I know her better than you do, and she would do anything to injure me. I know that I am not a good man, but I will do all in my power to make you happy."

"I trust you," she said, softly; "nothing shall make me doubt you again;" and we walked, in silence, towards the house. Before we said good-night, I made Maud promise to keep the matter quiet until the week was up; "for then," I said, playfully, "I shall know my fate."

I was greatly surprised to think how anxious I was for a marriage that seemed so distasteful to me the day before. "It is her very unwillingness," I thought. "If she had been more eager to accept me I might not think so much of it."

But it is ever so. Human nature will always be thus—people always longing, striving for something beyond their reach; and if perchance they attain the coveted object, it instantly loses its greatest value.

At the end of the week I won a shy consent to my proposal, and I thought it best to inform my father at once. He seemed to be expecting it, and congratulated me warmly. "You are a lucky boy," he said, "to win such a wife."

Mrs. Rogers took the matter coolly, and said

something about being very glad. But there was no answering gladness in my heart, for I knew her deceitful ways.

"You tried to turn Maud against me," I said to her one day; but she only gave a sneering laugh.

"I believe," I said angrily, "that you wanted to get rid of the girl."

"Perhaps so," she said, knowingly. And, in after years, I knew that it was so. When she thought that I would not marry Maud, she planned to make her life miserable, and so drive her from her home.

We arranged to have the wedding take place early in August. It was to be private, on account of Mr. Waters' death, and only a few distant relations were notified. We all spent the summer months at a fashionable seaside summer resort, and Maud seemed very happy. I was very attentive to her, and gave her many costly presents. Afterwards I was glad to think it had been so, and that for a short time I had contributed to make her happy; and if at times the image of another face rose before me—a face with dark, haunting eyes that I had once loved—I thrust the memory from me, and no one guessed the unsatisfied longing and deep yearning of my heart.

My father was in great glee at the approaching wedding. He arranged for me to have a yearly income, that I might not be dependent on my wife's bounty. Poor Maud, in her loving trust and confidence in me, had given me the management of her wealth. This was the worst thing that she could have done. Money had always led me into evil; and with wealth at my command I would surely go to ruin.

With the first of August came our wedding day, and nature seemed to have put on her fairest aspect to usher it in. Never did the sun shine brighter, or the birds sing sweeter, the flowers breathe choicer perfumes than they did on that morning. "Surely," I thought, "it is a good omen, and our future will be as fair and cloudless as yonder sky. Alas! how could I foretell the trouble that was in store for us; how could I see into the dark vista of futurity and read there the misery that was to come?

CHAPTER VI.

MARRIED LIFE.

WEDDINGS are an every-day occurrence, and are so familiar to every one that I think it useless to describe mine. We started for Paris the same day, and after spending two months in travelling we returned to New York and took up our abode. It was the worst place I could have chosen, for it was filled with old associates, old haunts, and old memories.

My old friends were not long in finding me out, and they began inviting me around. I soon neglected my home and sought amusement with them. At first Maud did not mind this, but after a time the cruelty of my neglect began to dawn on her, and she would remonstrate with me, and ask me where I spent my time. I would always have some excuse ready, and gradually her loving trust in me began to fade. It would have been better if I had told her all my weakness and temptation, for she might have saved me even then; but I chose my own path, and day by day we drifted further and further apart. I saw that my marriage had been a mistake, a grievous mistake, that could not be rectified, and the knowledge of it embittered my life.

I soon began squandering my wife's wealth. Some of it went to pay gambling debts; some of it was spent on pretty women. My own income I considered a mere trifle, and spent it as soon as I got it.

A life like this brought very little happiness. Maud soon saw that she had been deceived in me; that I was far from being the hero she had thought me. We had no tastes in common; she had her friends, I had mine; she amused herself with others, so did I. But it soon began to tell on her health; she grew thin and pale, and was but a ghost of her former self.

I will pass over the first year of such a life—a year during which I grew worse instead of better. Retribution, however, was soon to overtake me, and I would suffer as I had sinned.

One afternoon I was seated alone in the library, trying to read. I had been out till dawn the day before, and was suffering from a severe headache. Maud was downstairs in the drawing-room entertaining my father and his wife, who had come to pay us a visit. So engrossed was I with my miserable thoughts, that one of the hired girls entered and spoke to me twice before I noticed her.

"What is it?" I asked, at last perceiving her.

"Your father wishes to see you downstairs," she said; and I arose, languidly, and descended, mentally wishing my father at his own home.

When I entered the drawing-room, an excited group stood before me. At one end of the room Mrs. Rogers was supporting the half-fainting form of my wife, and in the centre of the room my father stood, confronting a tall, shabbily-dressed woman.

"What does this mean?" I cried. At the sound of my voice the woman turned, and I recognized the once pretty features of a young girl with whose affections I had seriously trifled some months before. I had almost forgotten the affair, until she stood before me like some dread accuser.

"Villain!" she cried, "I have tracked you at last."

"What do you want, girl?" I said, angrily. "If it is money ——"

"What!" she exclaimed. "Money! will money bring back my lost girlhood, my lost home? Aye, lady," she said, turning to Maud, who had sunk helplessly into the nearest chair, "once I was pure as yonder flowers that bloom unblemished, until he crossed my path and flattered me with his promises of love; and, innocent of the world and the wickedness of man, I listened and I fell. For his sake I left my happy home, my aged father and the loving friends of my childhood. For his sake I would have sacrificed my soul; and in return, he offers me money! But he soon tired of his pretty plaything—tired, as he will one day tire of you, lady, for his guilty nature cannot love. When I learned the truth, my whole being rose in rebellion against such a cruel wrong, and I swore to be revenged. Even now that I have destroyed the peace of his home I am not satisfied, and I will not rest until he has become, as I have, a homeless, friendless wanderer."

"Speak, Arthur," Mrs. Rogers exclaimed, crossing over to where I stood, the picture of despair. "Why don't you order her from the house? the creature must be mad."

"No, lady, I am not mad," the girl said in a

choked voice. "Perhaps, did you suffer the misery that I have suffered, you would indeed be mad. Sometimes I wonder that I am not so. You are a woman, with a woman's heart, a woman's instinct, you can pity me." She laid one thin hand on Mrs. Rogers' arm for an instant, but that worthy drew back with an affected shudder, as if there was contamination in the touch.

"How dare you?" she hissed in an angry tone.

But the poor, wronged creature was equal to the occasion. Drawing herself proudly up, she said in vibrating tones, "And who are you that I am not fit to touch? You think yourself mighty fine, do you not? You imagine yourself a lady because you have fine silks and jewellery, yet I, in my rags, am your equal, and," she added, "were you the queen of the universe, and I but the veriest wretch of all nature's creation, still would I think myself as good as you. But," she went on in softer tones, "why should I seek your pity? why should I need your help? soon I shall be beyond the reach of human aid Perhaps, ere another day shall dawn, aye, and perhaps ere yonder sun shall set, I will have sunk into oblivion 'neath the angry waters that are ever ready to engulf the wretched; then your pity cannot help me; then I shall have peace. Keep your money," she added, sternly, as my father offered her some. "Of what use is it to me?"

She turned and groped her way towards the door, and then paused and looked once more to where I still stood. "As for you," she hissed, "the author of my misery, may Heaven's bitterest curse descend upon you, and on your children; aye, and on your children's children! May your life be as miserable as you have made mine! May you die, as I shall die, comfortless, cheerless and alone!" Her voice died away faintly, and she was gone.

My father followed her into the hall, and I left the room by another door, for I felt just then as if I could not meet Maud's reproachful gaze; one glimpse of her sad face had told me that her trust in me was gone for ever.

I seized my hat and hurried from the house, to seek diversion with my companions amidst the gaiety of the large city, for I wanted to forget the unpleasant scene I had just gone through. No matter how hard I strived, I could not efface the memory of the white, despairing and reproachful face of the girl I had wronged. What a contrast, I thought, in this creature and the pretty maiden I had known her. Then she was a gentle, loving girl, in the bloom of youth, just entering the borderlands of womanhood, the pride and joy of her aged father, the sunshine of her home. Yet misery had brought about this change, transforming the loving, trusting maiden into the wild, despairing woman. And then I thought of Maud. She had blindly trusted me. and I was slowly, but surely, crushing all joy and beauty out of her young life. Better for her if she had never seen my face; now she will not care if she never sees me again. I thought, bitterly, of how I had lost all right to her love and confidence; but I had yet to prove the depth of a woman's love, the strength of a wife's devotion.

At this period of my life, I must have been surrounded by evil spirits who were trying to drag me down into the lowest depths of depravity and sin, for on all sides evil tempted me; and in the weakness of my soul I listened to the subtle voices that flashed like lightning through my brain. Remorse fled into the obscure mists of eternity, and evil reigned supreme master of my soul.

"What do you care?" the voice seemed to whisper. "Let other people be miserable. As long as you enjoy life, what does it matter how many hearts you break? There is no hereafter; life is short; so why not enjoy it?" And I made up my mind to do so, and became hard and defiant.

It was not till very late that I returned home. All the inmates of the household had retired, and were lost in peaceful slumber—the reward of a pure conscience. Through the weary night I slept at intervals—an uneasy and broken slumber that brought me no refreshing rest; and in the morning light I awoke to find my father slowly pacing the floor of my room. We had a stormy interview that lasted some time, but little good resulted from it. "You are a disgrace to your name," my father said, passionately, "and, if you do not change your mode of living, Maud will have to sue for a divorce."

"Indeed!" I sneered, "perhaps it would be the best thing she could do, if it would bring her any happiness."

"Oh," he went on, "it is too bad that she ever

married you, for you are not worthy of such a wife. Even now she is ready to forgive and forget all, if you amend your life. Poor girl, she thinks she is partly to blame. She says she did not try hard enough to keep you at home. But I know better; it is your own evil nature that has caused all this misery."

"It was you and your wife," I retorted, "that first put the idea of this marriage in my head; and you tried hard to bring it about. Now that you behold the consequences, you wish to transfer the blame to me."

"Talk sense," he said, angrily. "I am going home this evening, but will return at Christmas; and if things are not different, I will bring Maud back home with me, and she will make her home with us."

"I wonder what your amiable wife will say to that," I replied. "I don't think she would approve of it; she was in such a hurry last year to get rid of Maud."

To this he did not deign any reply, but left the room, loudly banging the door after him. I did not see him again, for he left late that afternoon for home, accompanied by his wife. I was out when they left, and did not return home until the shades of night had already descended on the city.

Never did my residence look so homelike to me as it did that evening. The low easy chairs, placed invitingly around, gave a look of comfort to the drawing-room, while a genial warmth, mingled with the perfume of flowers, pervaded the atmosphere. Through the curtained doorway that led into another room came the soft strains of sweet music, and I stood in silence to listen. It was Maud, playing to herself in the darkness, and she seemed to be pouring forth her whole soul in a flood of sad melody.

Music had always impressed me, and often it seemed to sooth the throbbings of my spirit, and still the disquietude within me. I had often wondered what it was in music that appealed alike to the great and humble, to the ignorant and the wise. To me it was the greatest of human joys, lifting the enraptured soul above the cares of the weary world, and ennobling it with pure thoughts. The music suddenly stopped and Maud came softly towards me, laying her hand gently on my arm.

"Perhaps you would like to hear," she said,

"that I have provided a home for that poor girl that was here yesterday."

"It has nothing to do with me," I said, roughly.

She drew back, with a low sigh. "Will you not stay at home to-night?" she asked, after a slight pause.

"I have an appointment," I said, hurriedly; "I must go out again."

"It is always something to take you from home," she answered.

"I did not marry you to be ordered about like an overgrown school-boy," I retorted. "I will stay in on Sunday. I have so many friends who are always inviting me around."

"Do you never remember your home?" she asked. "I have been thinking," she went on, "that we ought to go away for a short time; it would perhaps make a change; I am tired of this."

"You can go, if you want a change," I answered. "I am going to remain."

She made no reply; she evidently saw that it was useless. The matter was dropped there, and the old life went on as before; the months lengthened into winter and Christmas was approaching, and still there was no change.

CHAPTER VII.

THE RETURN OF A LOST LOVE.

ONE evening I was just leaving home, and at the steps that led to the door I encountered the figure of a woman in the act of ascending.

"Who do you wish to see?" I inquired. "Mrs. Rogers is not at home."

"It is you I want," she replied. "Don't you know me?"

"Rose!" I exclaimed, "is it really you?"

"Yes," she answered. "I have tried hard to find you. I must be greatly changed, since you did not know me."

"Come in," I said, hastily, "out of the cold; my wife is at the opera, and will not be home for some hours."

She followed me into the library, and, in the glare of the gaslight, I saw that she had grown pale and thin, and was poorly clad—quite a contrast to when I saw her last. I drew a chair forward for her, and she seated herself with a weary sigh.

"Now," I said, "we can talk unmolested. First tell me why you answered none of my letters?"

"Your letters!" she cried, in well-feigned surprise, "what letters?"

"Do you mean to tell me that you never received my letters?" I asked, incredulously.

"No," she said, slowly, shaking her head. "I never heard from you since you left New York, and I came to the conclusion that you had forgotten me. I read of your marriage in the papers, and I tried to forget that I had ever known you."

"And I thought you were false," I said, bitterly. "I waited in vain for an answer to my letters, and, when none came, I thought you had married some one else. Oh! why did you not give me some token—some sign that you were still true to me?"

"I was sick for a long time," she answered. "After I threw up my engagement at the theatre, I went over to Canada, but could obtain no employment; and then I fell sick. As soon as I recovered, I returned here, and, as I was in want, and having no other friend to apply to, I thought of you. I saw you several times on the street, and followed you home the other evening; that was how I found out where you lived. I thought, perhaps, in memory of our old love and happy days together, you would assist me a little."

"Why, of course, my dear girl," I exclaimed. "Why did you not apply to me before? Do you not know how I have longed for a sight of your face?"

"Hush," she said, "remember you are married."

"Yes," I said, bitterly, "married but not happy. Did you think that such a marriage was likely to be a happy one?"

"Do you remember," she said, thoughtfully, "all our old happy days? How you used to love me! Then I did not know my own heart, but now I know that I love you."

"Don't!" I pleaded, "the remembrance of it grieves me; those days are gone forever; why recall them? Another now stands between us, and our love is useless."

I gazed at her with a look of untold misery. "O Rose," I added, "it is so hard to bear!

You were cruel not to have sent me some word of your love, some token of your constancy. If you had done so, all this might have been averted."

"It is our fate," she said, with a low sigh of regret.

"No," I said, as I rose and impatiently paced the floor, "I am not going to submit to this. There is divorce open to me, for I still love you, and cannot live without you. How often have I recalled our promises of love, our bright dreams for the future, now faded and gone."

"I must go," she said, rising hurriedly to her feet. "Your wife must never know of this visit."

"I will go with you," I said, hastily. "I intend to look after you now."

"How good you are!" she murmured, softly, as we went out together into the chill November air.

I soon secured her comfortable lodgings in a fashionable quarter of the city, and we parted with a promise to meet again the next day. But this was only the beginning of many meetings, and I often cursed the fate that separated me from the woman I still loved; for, at first sight of her, all the old love had returned with renewed force. I kept her amply supplied with money, dresses and jewellery; at times I forgot to be cautious, and would be seen with her driving on Broadway, or seated in the opera, under the public gaze.

Somehow the story was carried to Maud; and one morning at the breakfast table she broached the subject.

"What have I ever done," she said, sadly, "that you should show me such little respect?"

"What do you mean?" I asked, calmly. "What is the matter now?"

"How disingenuous you are!" she rejoined; "why, it is the talk of the whole city. You are frequently seen in company with another woman, while I, your wife, am neglected at home, to be pitied and talked of."

"You are too sensitive," I replied, calmly, "you should not mind what people say."

"And is this life to go on always?" she asked, impatiently. "Is there never to be a change?"

"Since you are so unhappy, why not sue for a divorce?" I rejoined.

"No," she said, with a shudder, "anything but that. I could not stand the public exposure of the court; and in the end what should I gain?

The woman is always the one to blame in a case of that kind. No matter how innocent she may be, the world finds fault with her. And," she added, "though my burden is a heavy one, I must bear it to the end."

I made no reply, but silently left the room; and, a few hours after, I was laughing and talking joyfully with Rose. I had now grown reckless, and I spent all my spare time in her society. She always greeted me with her sweetest smiles, luring me from the path of duty into the road of destruction. At last I grew tired of the deceptive life I was leading, and determined to break the chains that bound me, and flee to some unknown country with Rose. It took me some time to make up my mind to do this, for I needed money. Rose was very extravagant and spent money as if it was picked up, and I knew that I would have to be well supplied with it before I ventured on the contemplated step; so I patiently waited my chance, without a sting of remorse for the cruel wrong I was inflicting on my wife. I comforted myself with the idea that marriage was no marriage unless there was perfect love. "It is only with Rose," I thought, "that I can find happiness—Maud will be better without me." In after years I reviewed this part of my life with sadness. How often do we look back and sigh with regret for what might have been!

About this time a change took place in Maud which greatly astonished me. She became a Christian. Hitherto she had expressed no settled belief, and attended no church. Her life had been devoted to fashion and pleasure. Now she suddenly changed her way of living and became a member of a wealthy church in the locality of our home, and all her spare time was spent in visiting the sick and distressed. She made no secret of her belief, and would sometimes tell me her experiences. Once, she commenced to relate some sermon to me, but I interrupted her with an impatient gesture. "You may believe all that rubbish," I said sharply, "but don't expect me to listen to it. I may never believe there is any truth in Christianity, and you will soon awake to find that it is all false."

"Oh, no," she replied. "I have experienced the comfort of religion, and the joy of doing good. I feel sure of a state of existence beyond the grave."

"You have your head full of fancies," I replied; "you need not repeat them to me, as I never can be convinced of a future state."

Some time after this conversation Maud suggested bringing her clergyman to see me, but I flew into a rage and told her to let me follow my own path in life, and she could do likewise. She made no effort after this to reform me. I have thought since that she did not go the right way about it, or did not rightly understand my character.

The week before Christmas my father arrived, and he was awfully indignant when he heard of Maud's conversion.

"It is all your fault," he said to me, in anger. "If you had treated your wife with the respect due to her, she would not have joined the Church. All they want from her is her money."

"It is only a fancy, and pleases her," I said indifferently; "she will soon grow tired of it." I thought it strange that my father said nothing of the conversation we had together on his last visit. But though he said nothing, I felt that he watched me closely. Yet I managed to evade him, and contrived to spend many pleasant hours in the society of Rose.

One evening my father tried to prevent my going out, and an angry scene ensued. I told him, hotly, that I was my own master, and would go where I pleased, and do as I pleased. I then left the house, and sought Rose for comfort. She was looking unusually lovely, in an evening toilet of some bright color, and some of the jewels I had given her gleamed conspicuously on the rounded arms, and encircled the slender fingers.

"I am going away," I said abruptly. "I will leave New York next week."

She gave me a look of alarm. "Are you going to desert me?" she asked, sadly.

"Leave you, my darling!" I cried. "No—you must come with me; we will fly into Canada, and live happily there."

"Do you really mean it?" she exclaimed, "or are you only jesting?"

"No," I said, earnestly. "I have thought it over for some time, and have at last determined to fly." And then I pictured a new life for us in a new country. She listened joyfully to all my plans, and, before I said good-night, I had arranged a plan for flight in the following week.

A few days afterwards I quietly helped myself to a few hundreds of my wife's dollars, comforting myself with the plea that I had a just claim to them. With this, added to my income which had just come due, I intended to start some business in Canada. Everything was now arranged, and to me the days seemed to drag on slowly. At last the week came to an end, and on Saturday, as I was going out, Maud came to me in the hall, looking very pale and careworn in the dim light.

"Arthur," she said coaxingly, "you might purchase tickets for our Bazaar. Spend some money in the cause, even if you don't wish to attend it."

And I, knowing that I would be far away at the time in question, readily gave the required promise, though I could not help feeling what a villain I was for deceiving her; but it was only a momentary pang, which soon passed away, when I reflected that in a few days I would be alone with Rose, and know that she was mine at last.

I suppose by this time the reader looks upon me as a very grievous sinner; but spare me your judgment, for only he who beholds the struggles, the temptations of a soul—he alone can judge!

CHAPTER VIII.

FLIGHT.

The night was dark and dreary. Overhead huge clouds of intense darkness gathered and rolled across the angry sky, and in the distance one could hear the low raging of the wintry blast as it swept through the almost deserted streets. I hurried along, with well muffled figure and bent head, in the direction of Madison Square, where I had arranged to meet Rose; for it was the night we had appointed for flight. I found her anxiously waiting for me, and in a very short time we commenced our journey. I experienced a feeling of relief, with a sense of freedom, and embarked on the fatal step without a thought of apprehension for the future, or a pang of regret for the past.

We decided to stay in Toronto; and I furnished a house there, and looked around me for a safe investment for my money. In this I was not successful. I had no business capacity, and

I let things go on as they were. Funds soon began to get low in Rose's extravagant hands. In vain I remonstrated with her. She only laughed at me, and told me there was plenty more where that came from, and that I had a rich father to apply to. But in this I knew better than she did. I knew perfectly well that it would be useless to apply to my father. I should never again spend a cent of his money.

Some months passed by, and I began to awaken from the glamour that had been cast over me. I beheld many traits in the character of Rose that did not please me. In the first place, she was an arrant flirt, and gathered a miscellaneous sort of people at our house—people that I detested, one man in particular, a tall, dark foreigner whom I will call Latondal. I thoroughly hated him; he was always hovering around Rose; and something in their conversation led me to believe that they had known each other in earlier life, but I could never get Rose to acknowledge it.

As the months sped quickly onward, I began to grow curious as to how they regarded me at home. I had one friend in New York whom I knew I could trust, and who was sure to be well "posted" in all the news. So one day I wrote to him, and in a few days back came an answer which somewhat startled me. I read first, that I was regarded in the city as a monster of ingratitude and cruelty, and that I must have been a heartless wretch, bringing disgrace on an honored family and a stain on a spotless name. Maud was seriously ill, and, at the time the letter was written, she lay at the point of death. The news of my flight, coupled with the loss of her money, had produced a severe shock to her system, already weakened by the trials she had gone through.

I could not help being touched with remorse, and I told the contents of the letter to Rose, expecting some sympathy from her.

"If Maud dies, it will be our fault," I said moodily.

"Nonsense," she replied; "it might have happened if you had never left her; but she will get over it. People do not die so easily."

For once she was wrong. A day or two later I received a newspaper from my friend, announcing the untimely death of "Maud Waters, wife of Arthur Rogers, aged twenty-four." Rose was in the room, and I silently handed her the paper, pointing to the paragraph; but she took it in a cool manner. "There is nothing to prevent your marrying me now," she said indifferently; and I, disgusted with her selfishness, left the house, and went out into the evening air to try and calm my agitated thoughts.

"It is the second time in my life that I have been the indirect cause of death," I said to myself, bitterly. Then I recalled the many instances of Maud's kindness to me, and how basely I had repaid her. And then I remembered the promise I had made her dying father, when the presentiment of this evil had overshadowed him —a promise never fulfilled, for I had badly befriended his orphaned girl.

"It is useless to recall the past," I thought sadly; "it is too late for atonement. I have gone too far in the way of sin;" and though the world believed that Maud died of a nervous fever produced by a severe shock, I knew that she died of a broken heart.

Every day after the news of Maud's death reached us Rose kept urging me for a speedy marriage; and in an evil hour I consented, little thinking of the misery it was to cause me in after years.

One dark, wet evening we were privately married in the minister's drawing-room. There were two witnesses present; and only one fact prevented entire happiness for Rose—she complained of not having enough money, and at the dull life she was leading, compared with the gay one she had been accustomed to.

"Why don't you write to your father for money?" she said to me one day.

"If you would be less lavish with your bills, there would be no necessity for asking anyone for money," I answered.

"What do you expect me to do?" she queried. "I must live. This place is so dull. I want some excitement."

"What more do you want?" I asked. "You are never satisfied. You have the best dress and the finest jewellery of any lady in the city."

"And what is the use of it all?" she grumbled. "I am sick of this place."

"Let us try Montreal," I suggested. "I might find employment there; for, unless money comes from some point, we are ruined."

At first she objected, but gradually gave in; and a few weeks later saw us installed in comfortable lodgings in Montreal. The city pleased me, but Rose did not like it; yet she contrived to make acquaintances, as she had done in Toronto, and I was surprised one day, on returning home, to see Latondal in our sitting room.

"How came that man here?" I asked Rose, after he had gone.

"He walked here," she replied defiantly.

"Don't trifle with me," I said, sternly. "I will not have any of your devilish tricks."

"Why, Arthur!" she said, with an affected laugh, for she saw my temper was rising, "what has come over you? Latondal is only a friend; I met him on the street the other day, and asked him to call. It is quite accidental; he is merely passing through the city."

I felt that she lied, but said nothing, resolved to watch quietly. Some instinct warned me there was something wrong.

I was unsuccessful in finding employment. I searched and advertised day after day, but with no success; and I began to grow discouraged.

One day I returned home, tired and weary, after a vain search. "I must be reaping the harvest of my sin," I thought wearily, for I had never felt so sad and downhearted. "Everything seems to turn against me; and even Rose, from whom I expected so much, is careless and indifferent how much I suffer, so long as she does not want for anything."

Our rooms were deserted when I entered, Rose had evidently gone out in a hurry, for things were scattered carelessly around. "Poor girl," I reflected sadly, "she will never be able to live in poverty; for her sake I must do something. Even now she does not realize how nearly beggared we are."

My eyes fell on a sheet of paper that lay on the carpet at my feet. I stooped, mechanically, and picked it up, and was surprised to find that it was a letter in my own handwriting. "Where in the world did this come from?" I muttered, beginning to read it; then, with a start, I crushed it in my rage, for it was the very first letter I had written Rose when I had first parted from her in New York. "She has deceived me," I groaned, for she had told me that she had never received any of my letters. "How can I ever trust her again! What was her motive!" I wondered. "Why had she denied ever having heard from me? I will find out," I cried excitedly. "I will know her reasons."

The sight of the letter had recalled to me all my anguish at the time it was written, when I had thought Rose was lost to me forever. I felt now as if I should go mad. The knowledge of her unworthiness crushed me; and, at the same time, I felt as if I deserved all I was suffering for the way I had treated Maud, who had been worthy of a better fate. The sting of remorse again entered my soul, and I saw my conduct in a new light.

I think, of all human sentiments remorse is the worst, for it embitters the soul and wrings the mind with anguish.

> "Lives there a man so firm, who, while his heart
> Feels all the bitter horrors of his crime,
> Can reason down its agonizing throbs;
> And, after proper purpose of amendment
> Can firmly force his jarring thoughts to peace?
> Oh, happy, happy, enviable man!
> Oh, glorious magnanimity of soul!" *

Even while these thoughts oppressed me, the door opened and Rose entered. There was a tender light in her liquid eyes, and a happy

---

* Burn's Remorse.

smile just parted the crimson lips. "Can it be possible," I thought, "that underneath this mask of loveliness there exists a heart of deceitfulness and sin!"

"See here," I said sternly, handing her the crushed letter, "this belongs to you: I found it on the floor."

She took it carelessly, and glanced at the writing; then I saw her color change and the smile die away—but for a moment—then, with an effort, she recovered her self-control.

"I suppose you have read it," she said defiantly.

"As I wrote the letter, there was nothing wrong in my reading it. And now perhaps you will explain your motive for deceiving me. Did you not tell me that you never heard from me after I left New York?"

"Would it do any good if you heard the truth?" she said, with a sneer.

"I would hear the truth," I answered; "my suspicions are dark enough. Why did you tell me that you believed me false, when all the time you knew differently? I once believed you above such deceit."

"And who are you to talk of deceit? Did

you not deceive your wife? and, after robbing her, desert her and leave her broken-hearted?" she said.

"Stop!" I cried; "you are going too far; I almost forget you are a woman, and that I once loved you."

The misery in my heart must have been reflected in my countenance, for her laughter rippled forth, and I knew it was in mocking derision at my anguish. She came towards me like some beautiful, gliding serpent.

"Poor fool! did you think I ever loved you?" she hissed,—"I, who might have had the United Kingdom at my feet! Men flattered and worshipped me for my beauty, but there was only one who ever touched my heart, one alone whom I could acknowledge for my master; but he scorned my love—he was too good and noble to love a woman such as I was; yet I tried hard to win him, and when I saw it was all in vain, I determined to be revenged. It was at this time that you appeared on the scene, and you were useful to me in many ways. Your money helped to bring me the things I loved, but I never intended to marry you; and when you left New York I thought I had seen the last of you. I received your letters, but determined to take no notice of them. The man I loved was then in Canada, and I followed him here to find I was too late; death had come before me and claimed him; he was beyond my reach—lost to me for ever—and I found that I was alone and friendless in a strange city. I was sick for a while, and when I recovered I returned to New York. I heard that you were married, and I made up my mind to see you, for I thought through you I could again obtain some help. The rest you know. I lied to you for my own good."

I raised my head and glared wildly at her.

"And it was for you I left my home, deserted a loving wife," I said sadly. "Well, I hope you are satisfied with your work; and if some day you hear of me as committing some dreadful, awful crime, then remember that it was you who made me what I am!"

She made no reply, but went into the next room; and I left the house and went out into the evening air, for I felt as if I was going mad. I knew that my sins had been great, but my punishment seemed more than I could bear.

CHAPTER IX.

RETRIBUTION.

As I tried to still the throbbings of my agitated brain, I wondered if all the world was full of evil, if there were no good people in existence. Suddenly the remembrance of my mother flashed through my whirling brain. She was good! And then Maud—what a good woman she was! Yet these two were Christians. If there is a God, He must be good! But how was I to find Him out—that unknown God? How was I to reach Him? Where could I find proof of His existence? "O ye heavens! can you not speak and tell me if there is a God?" I silently murmured. "And yonder cloud—if it could but move, would I behold a world of glory behind it? No, it is all a mistake! If there is a God, He is not for me; it is too late for me to seek Him."

And then my heart grew bitter against Rose. "But why should I mind her?" I thought.

"She is not worth my anger." Yet I could not banish the recollections of the old happy days when I thought she loved me, and when I believed her the fairest and purest of earth's creatures. But I was dazzled by the outside surface; I could not see beneath and read the faults and weakness of the soul. "What have I left to live for?" I asked myself in my misery; "if I were to die to-night there is not one living creature who would care—not one who would drop a silent tear to my memory."

For an instant I contemplated taking my own life; and then I banished the idea, as I thought that Rose would not care—perhaps would only laugh at me for my folly! So I determined to live on, even if it was nothing but misery—there was still a chance for a new life. That night I wrote a long letter to my father, in which I told him all. I did not spare myself in any way: I told him how Rose had led me on, deceiving me from the beginning; and then I asked him, as a favor, to send me some money, —for I had heard of a business chance, but needed a small capital. I only asked it as a loan, for I was sure of being able to return it, as I intended commencing a new life.

How anxiously I awaited a reply, and how long the days seemed to drag out their length! I knew that all my future depended on the answer I should receive. I had it addressed to the post office; and every day I went there, only to return disappointed. But it came at last, and, as I recognized my father's writing, I could not repress my agitation. "What did it contain?" I wondered, as with trembling fingers I tore it open. After briefly glancing at it, I saw that he had simply taken the letter I had sent him and returned it without a word of comment. He seemed determined to ignore my existence; and, though I made no outward sign, I felt crushed and bewildered with the disappointment I had received, for I felt as if my last hope had vanished—I was indeed friendless.

"It is only what I might have expected," I thought, wearily; "he will never forgive the past."

I returned homeward sadly, for I felt that I must tell Rose we were ruined; and yet I shrank from it—for, although she had deceived me and spoiled my life, she was the last creature left for me to cling to.

I well knew what a scene there would be when she heard the truth. Our rooms had a lonely, deserted look when I entered, and, although the April sun beamed brightly in, I shivered with the cold; a nameless dread had taken possession of me, and I could not shake it off. I looked around for Rose: she was not in, but I found a note, in her writing, on the table. I opened it, with wildly-beating heart, and read the following:—

"Dear Arthur,

"I think, after what passed the other evening, we are better apart. I fly with one who loves me better than you ever did, and with whom I hope to be happy. Do not try to follow me; it would be useless; and I hope you will learn to forget your lost

Rose."

And that was all—not a word of regret for the misery she had caused me; not a word of sorrow for the life she had spoiled! I looked sadly through the deserted rooms, and found that she had taken everything of the least possible value with her—selfish to the last. "Is it not a just retribution?" I asked myself. For her sake I had sacrificed all that would have made life dear to me—my home, my wife, and my father's respect; and now, in the hour of my greatest need, she had left me, penniless, friendless, and alone.

A sudden longing for vengeance took possession of me. I crushed her letter under my feet, and cursed her aloud in the bitterness of my rage. I well knew that it was with Latondal she had flown. "I will find them both, and kill them," I muttered through my set teeth; and I left the house determined to hunt them down.

A shower of rain had fallen and passed away, and the sun again shone out brilliantly, causing the raindrops on the branches of the trees to sparkle like countless diamonds. The streets were thronged with gaily-dressed people, and I vaguely wondered if anyone else was as miserable as I was. My first intention was to inquire at the railway station, to see if I could find trace of anyone answering to the description of those I sought. I hurried along westward on St. James street, and at one of the crossings I had to pause, for quite a crowd had gathered around a break-down—of an express or something—right in the middle of the road. Suddenly there was a shout from the crowd, and, turning round, I perceived a startled horse advancing at a great rate, dragging a shattered dog-cart after him, in which a lady was seated holding on like grim death. In an instant I comprehended her danger, for the frightened animal would inevitably come into collision with the broken-down express that lay in his road. As it dashed onward I sprang forward and stood in its path; and, as soon as it came near enough, I made a spring and grasped the bridle.

There was a sudden, swerving motion, and the shouts of the by-standers sounded dimly in my ears; there was a heavy thud, as I was thrown violently to the earth, where for a moment I faintly struggled with a sensation of weakness, and then all became a blank.

O blessed unconsciousness, that saved me from an awful crime and from a murderer's fate! for my brain, that had been working with thoughts of hatred and vengeance, was now still and senseless, and I knew nothing of what followed. I had a dreamy sensation of being lifted, and for a long time afterwards I seemed to lie enshrouded in a gloomy darkness. Then I fancied myself in a blaze of glaring light, from which I vainly tried to hide; and then, with a struggle, I opened my aching eyelids, to find that it was the mid-day sun shining full upon me.

"Where am I?" was my first thought, as I tried to collect my scattered senses. I gazed around me in bewilderment, for every thing was strange to me. I was lying on a soft, white bed in the centre of a large, rose-tinted room. Bright flowers were prettily arranged on a table beside my bed, and through the half-opened window came the soft, gentle spring wind, laden with the balmy perfume from the freshly-budding trees. I tried to rise, but fell back helpless. There was a slight noise, and I saw the door open and a lady enter. She was a stranger to me, yet something about her attracted my attention. She was not beautiful, but there was a look of nobleness about her—an expression of holiness and purity that told of a lofty soul. Her eyes were of a soft, dark grey, and filled with a gentle, tender light as they rested on me.

"Who are you?" I asked, in a weak voice, "and how came I here?"

"Hush!" she said softly, and her voice sounded like music in my ears, "you have been very ill, and you must not talk now—you are too weak." She gently raised my head and pressed to my parched lips some cooling draught, which I eagerly drank and then sank back exhausted.

This feeling of weakness was new to me, and it seemed strange that I, who had been so strong, was now as weak and helpless as an infant. A drowsiness came over me which I could not resist, and I fell into a refreshing slumber that lasted until night.

When I awoke, my brain was much clearer, and I looked around for the lady who had so greatly attracted me in the morning. She was not in the room; there was only an old gentleman—a venerable looking man—who was quietly reading by the aid of a subdued light. On perceiving that I was awake, he arose and came towards me.

"I am glad to see you better," he said heartily. "I have to thank you for saving my daughter's life. But for you she might now be lying cold in death, and I have much to thank you for."

As he spoke it all came back to me—the scene where I had tried to stop the infuriated animal. How vividly I remembered that I was in search of vengeance! and I could not repress a groan as I thought of it.

"How long have I been here?" I asked, faintly.

"Over two weeks," he replied; "you received

a severe wound in the head, which caused a slight attack of brain fever."

"Rose is undoubtedly beyond my reach by this time," I thought, with a sigh. And then I wondered about the noble face I had seen in the morning. Was it real? or was it only some vision of my fever-distorted brain?

"I will leave you now," the old gentleman said, "but I will send Alice to you; she has been your devoted nurse all through."

"Who can Alice be?" I wondered, as he left me. I was not long left in doubt. She soon entered—a gentle, graceful figure, in her soft, grey dress—and I recognized the face that I had been thinking about, and wondered what it was about her that attracted me. Afterwards I knew that it was the very purity and loftiness of her soul that acted like a magnet on my guilty nature.

"You have been very kind," I said softly, as she came towards me, "to one who was a stranger to you."

"'I was a stranger, and you took me in,'" she quoted, sitting down beside me, "and have I nothing to thank you for? How can I look upon you as a stranger, when you saved me from a serious accident, and risked your own life in the act?"

"Ah!" I said, "then you were the lady who was seated in the dog-cart."

"Yes," she said with a shudder. "It was an awful time, and when I saw you go down under the horse's feet I was sure you were killed. As soon as you fell, several others came to my assistance. I had you brought here in a cab, and have tried in vain to find out your friends."

"I have no friends," I said sadly. "I am alone in the world."

"Poor man!" she said gently, "but now you will not say that; you must look upon my father and myself as friends."

I took her outstretched hand and grasped it warmly, for something in her manner inspired my confidence.

"If you will take me into your friendship, I shall be so glad," I murmured; "and some day, if you will kindly listen, I will tell you the story of my life, and how it is that I am friendless."

"I would like it," she said, softly. "I too have had my trials: death has taken many loved ones from me; yet I look forward to the time when we shall be united, where there is no more sorrow—no more death."

I could not help smiling at the blindness of her faith.

"Do you believe in another life?" I asked. "Do you really believe there is a God?"

She regarded me for an instant in silent amazement.

"Don't talk like that," she said, with a shudder. "You cannot be in earnest—of course I believe in a God, and in a future life also; if I did not, I believe I should go mad."

"And yet," I said with a sigh, "I cannot believe it. I have tried and found no foundation for it—no proof."

"It is too bad," she said, with a sigh; "you have missed a great joy and comfort in your life. But God does all for the best; I think you were sent here for a purpose."

I thought, sadly, of my past life—so full of sin—and was silent.

"We will speak of this some other time," she said; "you are tired now, and I will leave you"—and, with a smile, she left me.

But I was now comforted and cheered, for I felt that I was no longer friendless and alone;

and there were still prospects of a new life. The old thoughts of hatred and revenge had vanished. I did not dare to think of Rose, but longed to be something better, nobler, than I had been. I wanted to be worthy of the trust of my new friends.

Is it ever reached—this striving for perfection? Not on earth; only when the cold mists have vanished, and the shadow of death has passed, then is that perfect, glorious peace reached!!

I fell asleep—a sweet, dreamless sleep that lasted till day-break. I soon began to recover my strength. In the pure atmosphere around me I saw how I had wasted my life, and I found all the old temptations powerless.

CHAPTER X.

MY NEW FRIENDS.

At the time of which I write there lived in the City of Montreal a man named Dalton, a man remarkable for his Christian charity, and of the highest mental culture. He was a widower, with an only child, Alice, the young lady I had rescued. Words of mine are inadequate to describe the goodness and pureness of her life. She possessed a character of the noblest, loftiest type, and I looked on in silent wonder at the life she was leading—so full of thought for those around her, so utterly forgetful of self: no stricken heart but felt the cheering comfort of her presence; no dying sufferer but felt the hopefulness of her prayers. It was a life of self-sacrifice and usefulness,—a life wherein she followed in the footsteps of the Master she professed. I see her now, as I saw her then, a pure and gentle spirit ministering words of hope to some despairing sinner, or soothing the anguish of some distracted brain; and again, leading some wandering sheep back into the Shepherd's fold.

Such were the people who taught me the meaning of friendship, and proffered me the hospitality of their home—me, the outcast and the sinner; and, day by day, their kindness to me was unlimited.

As soon as I grew a little stronger, Mr. Dalton promised me employment in his office, and I was determined he should find me straightforward and honest.

I now spent most of my time reclining on a sofa in the sitting-room. My chief delight was when Alice would come to me, ever cheering me with the brightness of her presence. One day she entered a little sadly, for she had just left a death-bed scene in the neighborhood, and the imprint of it seemed still upon her.

"You are wearing yourself out," I said to her; "you look quite pale and tired."

"I am a little tired," she said, wearily; "I hate to witness suffering. I have just seen a mother dying, surrounded by her weeping, helpless children; and I have been wondering why it is that God sometimes takes away those who are wanted on earth, while those who are despairing, and oft-times praying to die, live on."

"Yes," I replied, "that is one proof that there is no God: the world is so full of suffering and sorrow. If there was a God, He would not be so cruel. I am only human, yet I could not listen unmoved to all the despairing cries of the human race."

"Hush!" she cried, shrinking from me, "do not try to instil your miserable doubts into my soul. There is a God; I know it, feel it, and will yet prove it."

"If I could ever learn to believe in Him, it would be from you," I answered; "all you could ever teach would be good; still my doubting heart cries out for proof. How is it that you trust so blindly? What proof have you, for instance, that there is another life beyond this?"

"An instinct," she replied. "If I had no Bible, there is a something within me which I feel can never die. Even the poor Indian, in his savage, untaught ignorance, feels this instinct when he speaks of his happy hunting-grounds. How could I bear to think of the future, so ageless, endless, and of the millions of souls that have lived and passed away, if I thought there was no Supreme Being who governed all!"

"But," I persisted, "even if your Bible be true, it proclaims Him to be an unjust God. You believe Him omniscient: if so, He knows the sins and crimes a man is to commit when he is born; yet for those very sins that man is condemned to eternal punishment. Think of the countless thousands of people living in poverty and vice, miserable in life, yet dreading death,—for they are taught to believe that nothing but doom awaits them."

"You are wrong," she said quietly; "the same Bible that speaks of eternal punishment also speaks of forgiveness; man is sinful and always will be so, and 'the wages of sin is death'; yet, through the merits of Christ, all can be pardoned."

"That is another mistake," I interrupted; "there never existed such a Man; He is an impossible character."

"You are talking of something you don't understand," she replied to me: "He is the most perfect and purest of characters—perfect God and perfect man—and the day will come when you will acknowledge Him."

"You are so good," I murmured; "I wonder that you don't despise my ignorant sneers."

"I am not good," she said; "I may have been born with fewer wicked passions than you. If there is no temptation to struggle against, it is easy to be good; but he who conquers sin and daily struggles with the promptings of evil, and commands a victory over self—he is worthy of being called good."

I made no reply. Her words struck me forcibly. I felt as if she wished me to struggle with my doubts of Christianity. Yet I knew how useless it would be; nothing seemed to convince me. I would have given much to be able to say to her, "Thy God shall be my God, and I will serve Him;" but I could not do this—not unless I deceived her, and I was man enough to shrink from that.

Every day after this we spent a short time together, talking over religion and Christianity. I was very obstinate, but she had great patience, and gradually led my darkened mind into the truth, sometimes taking lessons from nature, sometimes from her Bible, which was an inseparable companion.

One fine, peaceful Sunday, Mr. Dalton proposed that we should ascend the mountain and view the city from its summit. To this I eagerly assented; and together we drove up, and alighted when we reached the top. Alice and I sauntered off to find a favorable point of view, leaving Mr. Dalton conversing with a friend he had met.

"See!" Alice exclaimed, "behold the scene before you, and tell me how you can say there is no God! How can you account for this creation—the exquisite coloring of the landscape and the abundance of life around us?"

It was indeed a scene worthy of admiration. Below us lay the city, calm and quiet in the evening mists; and onward the waters of the St. Lawrence flowed, numerous islands resting peacefully on its bosom; while on the other side spread the blue outline of mountains.

"Is there nothing in this," my companion asked, "that appeals to your soul? Is there no inspiration in the lovely landscape? nothing in the soft sighing of the summer wind that creates in your soul a longing for a nobler life? To me it is the surest proof of God's existence. I see His handiwork all around me in the varied year, whether in the soft splendor of summer, or the hoary majesty of winter; and if He has made this passing world so fair, how much better must that home be that He has in store for us?"

"I wish I had your faith," I answered; "how blindly you trust!"

"No, not blindly," she replied; "I trust because I believe, I do not understand how anyone can be so doubting; even the very birds seem to be singing the praises of God, and my heart goes out in silent admiration—first to nature, then on to nature's God."

"If there is a God, why is there so much misery in the world?" I asked; "why is He cruel?"

"You are mistaken," she answered; "we must not question His divine will; whatever He does is for the best; 'whom He loveth He chasteneth.'"

"And do you believe," I asked, incredulously, "that man, after suffering misery in this world, is to be eternally punished in another life? Take myself, for instance—do you think I merit eternal punishment for those doubts that I cannot help?"

"No," she answered; "for I believe they will all pass away, and you will regret them. You have told me that you were brought up away from home—among unbelievers—and without any loving voice to teach you right from wrong. I think that you are not responsible for being so doubting. I wish you would study the life of Christ; it would help you to understand what now seems so dark."

"No," I said, "if anything ever convinces me, it will be your teachings. I have read the life of Christ, and it made no impression on me; I looked upon it as fiction—the offspring of imagination."

"Oh!" she said, softly, and a holy light seemed to illuminate her countenance, "I love to picture Him in His earthly life, partaking of our human nature, yet God, suffering the sneers of man. Again, I see Him treading the plains of Galilee—a man of many sorrows; yet, although rejected by man, the world around Him knew He was no impostor. At His word the tempests hushed their angry tumult, and the wild waves ceased their surging when He murmured, 'Peace, be still.'"

I made no answer.

"And," she continued, "you say that His life is the result of imagination; but no man living at that period could have imagined such a pure and holy character. His very doctrines proclaimed Him God. The prophets of old fell from grace, but in Him there was found no sin."

Mr. Dalton here joined us, and we retraced our steps, for night was already casting her mantle of darkness over all the landscape.

I was silent during our homeward drive; something within me seemed too deep for utterance. I retired early to my own room. Alice had gone to church.

"What has come over me?" I asked myself in the solitude of my room, as I stood at the open window gazing into the darkness. Once I would have laughed at the notion of being a Christian; now all is different. "If there is a God, why have I not known Him?" I thought, sadly, "why has He forgotten me? and if there is another life, how can I enter it? How can my guilty soul float out alone into the ageless, endless eternity?" It was all too much for me; I could not grasp the truth; I could not yet believe.

Like a flash, the image of a pure face rose before me—a face illumined with a heavenly light, the soft, grey eyes shining with unspoken thoughts that indicated a lofty soul. I started as the truth came suddenly upon me. I loved her! Yes, strive as I would, I could not hide the truth; I, the outcast, the guilty, sin-stained wretch, dared to love her, who was as far above me as light above the darkness. It was no passing fancy, no fragile love to be easily cast aside. I loved her with all the strength of my manhood, with a love that could never die. And oh! the misery of the thought: I was not free to love; Rose was, no doubt, still living, and she was still my wife. I think if it had been in the old days, and any other woman but Alice, I would have wooed and won her, and said nothing of Rose. Now all was changed; the very purity of her nature protected her. "I might as well try to grasp yonder star in the heavens," I thought, "she would despise me, if she knew I had dared to love her. But no, she would only pity me, perhaps even pray for me." It was the bitterest hour of my life. I cursed the fate that brought me no joy, no peace in life. And then softer thoughts came to me. I knelt down, alone in my misery, at the open window, and pillowed my aching head. "O God!" I cried, "if you exist, why have you deserted me? why is my life so full of anguish? why have you implanted this love within me, when it can only result in misery?"

All through the long, still hours of the night, I remained there, struggling with my anguish, fighting the hardest of all battles—a war with myself. In that struggle all the evil within me seemed to die. I felt as if my love had created within me a purer, better spirit; and that henceforth I would live to be worthy of it.

O Thou great God, who dost behold all the heartfelt yearning of an anguished soul, I think in that hour Thou didst pity me; I think some spirit of mercy, direct from Thee, whispered to my wounded heart sweet words of hope!

And as the morning dawned the good within me conquered. I would go away, far from this peaceful spot where I had been so happy. I knew it would be useless to live in her presence and try to hide my love; so it was best that I should go; and she should never know how dearly I had loved her, for the knowledge would but cause her pain. I knew my life would be dreary without her. I should be sure to relapse into the old, guilty life. But no, the very memory of her would be enough to restrain me. She would be my guiding star; and for her sake I would lead the life she had taught me.

CHAPTER XI.

BLIGHTED HOPES.

I HID my secret well, but it was weary work. I was loth to leave yet the scene where I had been so happy, and I lingered on through the summer months until the autumn leaves were falling.

One evening I had just returned home from work, for I was now employed by Mr. Dalton. I was silently thinking over the future, as I knew that this life could not go on much longer. I carelessly picked up an old newspaper from the table, and was startled to see my own initials heading a " personal " paragraph, which read as follows:

"ARTHUR R.—Forgive the past. I am alone and dying at the old place.—ROSE."

I felt the blood receding from my face, and a cold, death-like feeling swept over me. I looked at the date of the paper; it was a week old. What was I to do? At first I thought that I would tell Alice all, and ask her advice. Then I shrank from it, for I thought she would perhaps regard me with horror when she came to hear the recital of my life; she was so pure and good, she would not understand how I had listened to the voice of evil. I was tempted to take no notice of the "personal"; but just then Alice happened to enter the room. She looked so fair, so saintly, that at sight of her my better nature prevailed.

"Tell me," I said, turning to her, "if a man is deeply wronged, is he not justified in hating the one who has spoiled his life? Would you, if any one injured you beyond repair—would you forgive him?"

"I think so," she said softly, a look of surprise dawning in her grey eyes as she saw my emotion. "Take Christ for your example always; see the sublime purity of His life: He forgave those who wronged Him; and how can any one hate a soul that He loves! You know," she added, "that 'to err is human, to forgive is divine.'"

Her sweet words decided me, and I determined to see Rose and forgive the past—forgive, though in the end it would surely cause me pain.

It was Rose who had inserted the paragraph, of that I had no doubt; but I did not believe she was dying—that was only a trick of hers to entrap me. She was probably deserted by the partner of her flight, and sought to try and obtain aid from me. By "the old place" I surmised that she meant our former lodgings; and there I went without any delay. The landlady, a sprightly little Frenchwoman, received me with an agitated manner. "You are too late, sir," she said, as I entered.

"What do you mean?" I asked; "is Mrs. Rogers not here?"

"She was here," the woman answered; "she came to me about three weeks ago. She was very sick and I 'done' my best for her, but all in vain. She seemed repentant, and tried hard to find you."

"Do you know where she is now?" I interrupted.

"She left here in a dying state," the woman replied, "saying that she was going to some friends in Boston; and last week I received a letter stating that she was dying, and that is all I can tell you; she is probably dead by this time."

I asked for the letter, and she gave it to me. I lost no time, but went home and wrote to the address stated, for I was determined to know the truth. I wanted to hear whether I was free, or still bound to one I now considered unworthy of any man's regard. I wondered how I had ever been so foolish as to imagine I loved her. It was only an infatuation, a passing love, that I now regarded as a dream.

An answer came quickly to my letter, which put an end to my suspense. The writer was a stranger to me, and briefly informed me that my wife was dead. It never occurred to me to doubt the truth of this statement. I was only startled, for I had never thought of her dying, she had always been so full of life and seldom sick; and I could hardly realize that she, for whose smiles men had fought, and whose beauty women had envied, was dead. It is ever thus: the young and beautiful pass away, even as the old and feeble. It was strange to think of her as dead, her rich glowing beauty faded into nothing. Yet, mingled with the thoughts of her, came a sweet thrill to my heart, as I suddenly remembered that there was now no living barrier existing between Alice and me.

But could she, one of the purest and noblest of women, link her fate with mine—the guilty sinner?

I resolved to test her feelings towards me. She had ever been kind, patient and gentle with me; her sweet, innocent nature never suspected the deep love I entertained for her.

One evening, I strayed out into the autumn air. A slight wind was stirring among the vari-colored leaves of the trees, and many of them fluttered to the ground at my feet. I went into the faded garden, where the fitful moonlight was casting ghostly shadows. Here I resolved to await the coming of Alice. She had gone on some visit of charity, but I knew she would soon return. In this I was right; I soon beheld her coming towards me, and I stepped forward to meet her. She gave a start of surprise on seeing me.

"You!" she said, with the tender smile I knew so well.

"Yes," I answered, "I have been waiting for you; I have something to tell you."

"What is it?" she asked.

"Do you remember," I asked, "my once telling you that I would one day relate to you the story of my life? Will you listen to it now?"

She nodded her head in silent assent, and I began and told her all my past life, with its weakness and sin, the same as I have already described to the reader. I omitted nothing save the date of Rose's death; I merely told her that I had proof of that fact.

I half expected Alice to shrink from me during the recital of my crimes, but she never changed the sweet expression of her countenance.

"Now," I exclaimed, when I had finished, "you know what a sinner I have been; despise me if you will, but remember that I knew no other life. I had no one to teach me of that life the Christian leads. Will you be my judge, and tell me if I am beyond redemption?"

"Who am I?" she said, "that I should judge you? How could I know the conflictings of your soul—that soul so wondrous, created after God's image. Who but He shall dare to judge it?"

"But," I cried, "will you not speak some word of comfort to me? You always help me so much; you have already persuaded me that there is a God. I now believe in a Supreme Being who governs the Universe, but further than that I cannot believe."

"It will all come in God's own time," she answered. "He will one day banish all the doubts, and lead you safely into His eternal home."

"Ah," I said, in a despondent tone, "my faith is so weak; it is only you who can help me. I love you—fondly, devotedly love you! But why do you shrink from me? Are you angry because of this love which I cannot control? How could I help it? How could I live in the sunshine of your presence, and behold the noble self-sacrifice of your life, and not love you? Am I so despicable, so hateful in your sight, that you shrink from me in horror?"

"No," she replied, with a troubled look, "it is not that; but I have never thought of such a thing. I have planned out for myself a life so different, a life spent in the Master's cause, which I would live alone, caring for His wandering sheep, feeding His hungry lambs."

"Why alone?" I pleaded; "with you to help me, I could embrace your doctrines and accept your faith. We would work together, you and I, and we should be so happy; but," I added, sadly, "you do not think me worthy of your trust."

"You do not understand," she said, in a low tone: "I do not think you so bad; indeed, I have watched well, and I believe that you possess many noble qualities that only await development."

"Then," I cried in a voice of entreaty, "help me to attain a better life. You alone can save me. If you will not marry me, if you send me from you, I am lost."

She made no sign, but I saw that she shivered slightly, and she turned so that I could not see her face.

"Very well," I said, sadly. "I see that I am abhorrent to you. I will not trouble you again. I will go from you now, back to the old life, so full of sin and misery; and some day when you stand face to face with that God you profess to love, how then will you be able to answer for the soul you might have saved?"

I turned as if to leave her, but she grasped my arm; "Stay," she gasped; "for the present you have won; I stand amidst conflicting duty, —my own plans on one side, you on the other. I cannot bear to picture you back in the old life, lonely and cheerless. He who implanted that love within you, must have done so with a purpose, and I bow in deep submission to His will."

"My darling!" I cried in rapture; "you have made me so happy. You shall never repent those blessed words. You have given me something to live for; life seems no longer empty and cheerless."

"But you must not be too sanguine," she interrupted. "I cannot marry you while you are an unbeliever; no happiness would result from it. When you become an honest Christian, then you can speak to me of marriage."

"Is not that hope sufficient to sustain me?" I replied. "I will work so hard to be worthy of your trust. I will find no labor too difficult, no task too arduous, if in the end I can but win your love."

"I feel as if it will turn out all right," she replied. "I think that He who imposed this duty on me will bless it with success; and we can safely leave the future in His hands."

The hour was getting late and we went into the house. The days that followed were happy ones for me—the happiest I was ever to know on earth. There seemed no cloud to darken the brightness of the future. I studied hard to overcome my doubts about Christianity. Alice read much to me on the subject, and I had gradually come to believe in a God, though I could not yet believe in an eternal life. Sometimes in the solitude of the night I would argue the matter out with myself. "Was it possible," I asked myself, "that there were separate states of existence beyond the grave—one for the good, and one for the bad? If so, there would be only misery in such an existence. People separated from those they loved on earth—how could they be happy, knowing that their loved ones suffered?" If it was true, Alice would surely be among the good, and I cast among the worthless. "Was there any truth in it?" I wondered. "Was it possible that when I should resign this earthly body I should still exist, a conscious being, capable of enduring pain or experiencing joy? No, it could not be!" I believed that when a man died he became nothing—mingled with the dust.

Alice talked much to me about this doubt. "Why can you not believe?" she would say, sadly. "Surely, He who made us did not do so for this passing world. Of what use would it be to create souls if they were all to perish and become nothing!"

Poor girl, it pained her to see me so doubting; yet I could not help it. She now asked me frequently to accompany her to church; but, although I went, I did not seem convinced. I used to like much better to go with her on some mission of charity, which I invariably did, and in this way saw the different phases of life.

I began to hope that I was gaining favor in the eyes of Alice. I believed that she was not quite indifferent to me, and a sweet hope thrilled me as I thought perhaps I was gaining her love.

All this time I did not hear anything more of Rose's death. I had written twice, but received no answer. This I thought strange, and determined to go to the address stated in the letter I had received, and obtain particulars for myself. The winter had now set in, and Alice kept me very busy helping her to look after the poor.

One evening we had just returned from a long tramp through ice and snow, and were enjoying the genial glow of the bright fire.

"I feel unusually joyful to-night," Alice said to me in an undertone. "Let us have some music."

"Yes," I eagerly assented; "do sing some

of your sacred songs; they may awaken some responsive chord within my heart."

She selected "Rock of Ages," and seemed to pour out her trusting faith in the sweet words. I stood silent beside her; but when she came to the last verse, I could not help joining in the refrain, "Rock of Ages, cleft for me, let me hide myself in thee."

Before the last words died away, I heard the door open and some one enter, but did not turn round, thinking it was Mr. Dalton. Alice was the first to look to see who it was, and then I saw her rise with a surprised look. "What is it?" I heard her say: "did you wish to see me?"

Then I looked; and as I did so, I could feel all the joy within me die. It seemed to me as if everything around me was fading from my sight. A female figure stood just inside the door, with a mocking smile on her lips—a smile that sent an icy chill to my heart, for I knew it so well. I recognized her in spite of the ravages of illness, and the changes dissipation had made in her once beautiful countenance. I knew her in spite of the dishevelled hair, the worn-out garments. It was Rose, alive and standing in the flesh before me, ready to dash the cup of happiness from me.

"What do you want, my good woman?" Alice asked again.

"What do I want?" Rose repeated. "Ask him!" she added, pointing to me. "Ask my husband!" She seated herself in the nearest chair and gazed defiantly at me, while Alice, grown strangely white, looked from one to the other of us.

"Leave us," I said to her, hoarsely. "Leave me to deal with that woman; this is no scene for you."

"Yes, it is," she returned, quietly. "I think I understand it all; and I had better stay. Besides, this poor woman may need my assisttance; she looks quite faint. If you go downstairs you will find some wine in the diningroom; please bring some up; it will revive her."

Dear, gentle soul! she only saw a creature in distress, no matter how great her sin, how deep her crimes. Rose, with her pale, emaciated features, was still a fellow-creature who needed help.

I rose to comply with Alice's request. She had seen that I was in no mood to be trusted alone with the woman who had so cruelly wronged me, and thought by sending me from the room my anger would have time to cool. I let my eyes rest upon her for an instant, and I perceived, with a thrill of anguish, that she suffered; her clear eyes had in them a wounded look, that told of a sensitive soul apprehensive of suffering. Yet even as she met my gaze, she tried to smile bravely, as if bidding me be of good cheer. I knew that she suffered because I did, and the very thought of it was anguish to me. It was not of herself she was thinking, but of me. It crushed me to think that I, who fain would have crowned her life with every blessing, was the first to cause her sorrow.

Oh my darling! how trifling it all seems now, as viewed from the height of our superior wisdom! When we look back upon those earthly scenes so fraught with anguish, how little do they appear! and how we wonder they ever pained us!—of the earth, earthly and swiftly passing away. O ye people, who are in grief, in sorrow or misery, why do ye lament and mourn your fate? Know ye not that a change soon comes, and that for all ye suffer your reward shall be great? Not a silent tear, not an anguished cry but your God beholds; and His word changeth not. It was no vain promise that He made when He said: "Blessed are they that mourn, for they shall be comforted."

CHAPTER XII.

PARTED.

I FOUND the wine that Alice had sent me for, and returned with it, dazed and stupefied by the sudden blow that had fallen on my hopes. When I reached the half-open door the sound of my name caused me to pause, involuntarily. It was Rose speaking to Alice. "You do not love him," she was saying, "or you would not so easily give him up. If you will give me money enough to start a new life, I will go away and never trouble either of you again. You can marry him if you wish. I will be the same as if dead."

I listened for the reply, curious as to how Alice would receive this evil suggestion.

"Would you have me become as base and sinful as yourself?" was the reply. "You have formed a wrong opinion of me. If I loved him ever so dearly, still would I renounce him; he is bound to you."

"You are taking a very foolish view of the matter," Rose answered. "He will be only too glad to see the last of me. I know he is in love with you."

"There are many kinds of love," Alice replied; "there is that deep and holy love which passeth all understanding, and the pure love that lives forever,"—I waited to hear no more, but entered the room.

"Now," I said, sternly, "in the presence of the noble woman I love, I ask you why you have duped and tricked me?"

"I may as well tell you," she answered; "I see it is useless to hide the truth from you. When Latondal abandoned me, sick and friendless, I returned to our old lodging-house, thinking to find some trace of you, but all in vain. I remembered a friend I had in Boston, some years before, and to her I went. There I slowly recovered a little strength; and then came your letter of inquiry, and I told them to report me as dead. I thought perhaps you would marry again, and I could then extort an income from you as hush money; but I see I have appeared too early on the scene." A hollow cough interrupted her flow of words, and she looked weak and exhausted. "It is no use glaring at me like that," she said to me; "I have not long to live; and if I have sinned, I have suffered."

"If you only want money," I said, "here, take it and go, and never let me see your cursed face again."

"Hush!" Alice interposed. "How can you talk like that? Surely you, who have need of forgiveness, can forgive!"

I drew back with a shudder. "No," I said, in an undertone, "I cannot."

"Poor creature!" Alice went on; "if she should die to-night you would regret it."

"For your sake, my darling," I whispered; then, turning to Rose I held out my hand: "Here," I said, "I am willing to help you; I will see that you do not want for anything."

Words of this kind crushed her more than anger would have done; and, as Alice led her gently from the room, I saw the tear-drops glistening in her eyes.

For a long time after they left me I paced the floor in silent agony.

"Fool that I was," I thought, bitterly, "to dream that any joy or peace could ever enter my cursed life. Oh, that I were dead and free from all this misery!"

I cast myself helplessly into a chair. Something like a sob seemed to rise in my throat and stick there, as I thought of parting from Alice. Soft footsteps sounded on the carpet, but I did not lift my head; a gentle hand was laid on my arm, with a sympathetic touch—a touch that would have had power to recall me from the dead; it was Alice come to comfort me in my misery.

"Bear it bravely," she whispered; "God sometimes punishes sin in this world that the penalty may be lessened in the next."

"Don't talk to me of your God," I replied; "He has forgotten me."

"Don't say that," she pleaded; "have all my teachings been in vain? It would break my heart if you were to turn atheist again."

"What does it matter?" I answered; "I don't care now what becomes of me."

"But you must," she replied. "I think there are many happy days in store for you. Do you think I have not suffered also? Did you think I could lightly lose you just as you were beginning to be useful to me? But I have conquered it. I know that God does all for the best." I raised my eyes and gazed at her, and I saw that she had been praying; all the misery had died from her eyes, and instead they shone with the light of faithfulness and trust.

"Why need we be unhappy?" I said. "I will get divorced from that creature, and then we can be married."

"No," she answered, "that would be useless; though the laws of man would pronounce you free, yet in the eyes of God that woman would still be your wife."

"Don't remind me of her," I protested. "Let us forget her. Fly with me to some distant land. Don't be eternally thinking of a future. There is no other life. Why not be happy in this?"

Slowly she drew back from me, an expression of sorrow settling on her features; it was her first strong temptation, but she never wavered for an instant.

"Don't talk to me in that manner," she said, "or you will teach me to despise you. What have I ever done that you should think so little of me?"

Her whole attitude was so expressive of sorrow that I cursed my hasty words.

"Forgive me," I pleaded; "I am not myself to-night. Speak one word of forgiveness, and I will leave you and pass from your life forever."

Then she looked sadly at me. "Do you think that I would be any happier for that?" she answered: "I too suffer; yet I know that it is all for the best. If you will go to some friends of mine, I know that you will find a comfortable refuge. They are a clergyman and his aged wife. If anyone can make a Christian of you, it is he. If you will go to them, I will write at once; they live in Western Canada."

"What does it matter?" I said, in a despondent tone; "since I am to go from you, I don't care what becomes of me."

"Well, I will go and write to them," she answered; "you had better try and get some rest."

I almost laughed at the idea, as she left me. Rest! I felt as if I should never know any rest on earth again.

The next day Rose left for Boston, well supplied with money. She seemed overcome by the kindness shown her, and promised to lead a repentant life. I told her as soon as I was settled in my new home I would write to her.

Alice received a favorable reply to her letter, and it was decided that I should start the next Monday. She would have liked to have seen a complete reconciliation between Rose and myself, but I told her it was impossible; that it was better we should each work out repentance separately.

My last Sunday with the Daltons was a sad one. Alice gave me many good instructions, and promised to pray earnestly for me. Never shall forget our parting scene. It was a beautiful winter's morning; the freshly fallen snow sparkled and glistened in the rays of the sun; the whole landscape was completely covered with a mantle of white; even the branches of the trees were laden with it.

Alice stood in the doorway—a figure as pure and spotless as the snow around her—a brave smile resting on her features as she murmured "farewell."

"Farewell!" how sad the word, yet how different its meaning! To Alice it meant only a brief farewell.

"We will meet again," she whispered; "if not on earth, it will be in that other life where all is joy."

To me it meant farewell to all hours of peace, all moments of joy; farewell to the fairest and noblest of God's creatures, the woman I loved.

She had pressed her little Bible into my hand at parting, and I looked at it sadly. She had marked out several passages for me to study, and I determined to do so. One thing pained me deeply: she had told me not to write to her.

"I will hear of your progress from Mr. Austin," she said; "if in the end you conquer all your doubts, it will please me greatly."

I found my new home was in a rustic village, among a lot of true-hearted Christians. Something about it reminded me of my boyhood's home. Mr. and Mrs. Austin were a friendly old couple, and at once made me feel at home To Mr. Austin I told a portion of my life, and frankly recounted to him all my doubts on Christianity.

"Ah, my boy," he said, " they will one day pass away. I have met many like you, but in the end truth conquered."

I now began to lead a life that I knew would please Alice. Mr. Austin was old, and I helped him in many ways. Often the dreary night would find me a still watcher at some sick bed.

For miles around the people began to know me. I never prayed with them, but I would often read the Bible at some bedside; and the people grew to look upon me as a Christian. All doubt as to the existence of a God was now removed from me; it was the other dogmas of Christianity that I could not master. In that village home I learnt many lessons of patience and self-denial. No sin seemed to tempt me, for in that peaceful spot there lurked no evil. Mr. Austin was ever ready to help me with friendly counsel and advice. He it was who first awoke me to a consciousness of my danger. "Repent," he would say, "while there is time, for no man knoweth the day nor the hour of death's call."

I would listen silently to it all, pondering over each word. Oh, the burden of a guilty conscience! how I wrestled with the wild throbbing of my sinful soul! The wrongs I had inflicted on Maud rose vividly before my heated imagination, until it seemed to me that I was past redemption. Oft in the silent hours of night, visions would seem to float around me—visions of Maud, not with celestial brow nor crown of glory, for I believed it not; but I conjured her as of old, with sad face and reproachful eyes, that seemed to accuse me of being the cause of her untimely death.

Those were my darkest hours; yet, mingled with this misery, came sweet memories of Alice, like an oasis in the desert of my life. The time was when I could have cursed the fate that had thrown me in her path, since it was but to lose her when apparently won. Now I was glad that I had known her, glad to have loved her.

About this time I received a letter from Rose. By its contents I surmised that she was unhappy. The illness she was suffering from at our last meeting had terminated in consumption. I sent her all the money I could spare, and though I felt it was my duty to go to her, I could not do so just then—the wrongs of the past were too vividly before me.

Why is human nature so obstinate, I wonder? Thou blessed Creator of mankind, who dost implant in the souls of men passions which they cannot control, how wonderful is Thy patience! how forbearing Thy judgment! Here in the Spirit world is seen Thy perfection! Here in these spheres of knowledge is known Thy love!

CHAPTER XIII.

FREE AT LAST.

One morning I received a letter from Rose, and, after reading it, I concluded to go to her. "The end is approaching fast," she wrote, "and soon you will be free."

I knew if Alice were near me, she would bid me go; and for her sake I went. Ah, what a strange meeting that was! how different to what I ever expected! Rose, the dying, repentant sinner, was a different being to the woman who had wronged me; and, at sight of her suffering, all resentment died from my heart.

"It is so good of you to come," she murmured, faintly; "I did not expect it."

And now came a heavy trial for me. Day after day she would question me as to the life beyond—that life so dim and uncertain—upon whose borderlands she stood. Alas! what could I tell her? How could I comfort her?

"Once, in the long ago, I could pray," she murmured; "now, I have forgotten how."

Tenderly I read to her the story of Christ's love for sinners. How eagerly she grasped the truth, how readily she believed it all! "There is hope for me then," she would say; "surely He who was so meek, so patient, so humble, will forgive. I am no longer afraid. Christ, so kind, so good, will not desert a repentant sinner."

Poor trusting heart, no shadow of a doubt came to mar the tranquillity of her mind. She trusted in the Saviour's promises much more readily than I did. She believed, yet she had no proof beyond what I had read to her.

She spoke no more of a life beyond the grave. "I know there is one," she said. "What it will be for me I know not, but oh, the regret, the misery of the thought, that I have lived in vain!"

I lingered by her side for two or three weeks, patiently waiting for the end. It was pitiful to behold her suffering; yet, through it all she never murmured. Once she spoke to me of Alice. "When I am dead," she said, "I hope you will marry her; she is a good woman, and the first night I saw her, I perceived the contrast between us. Tell her I died trusting in the Master she loves."

The end came at dawn of the next day. I

held her hand in mine, and, at her request, I repeated the Lord's prayer. It was the first time I had truly prayed. As I did so, a flood of holy light seemed to illumine my soul, and I knew that I had found the truth at last. As I repeated the last words, a smile flitted over the dying features before me. Gently the angel of death loosened her weary spirit, and it fled. I stood beside her, silent and motionless, trusting that she had found the Saviour as merciful as He was represented to be; and as I stood there in the dim light and unbroken silence, I vowed to live a life of amendment in the future, and atone for each sin I had committed.

After a lonely funeral, I returned to Mr. Austin's; but not before I had placed a simple slab of white marble on the grave of her who, in spite of all her faults, was yet sacred in death. Strangers often view that lonely grave, and they know not that underneath it sleeps one of the most beautiful women the world has ever seen. Who shall judge her? Reader, surely not you, nor I! Can we not safely trust her to that Saviour who came not to call the just, but the sinner, to repentance?

For three long months I worked steadily on

with Mr. Austin. I would have liked to have gone straight to Alice, now that I was free to love her; but I contented myself with writing her a full account of what had happened, knowing that it would please her best if I waited and curbed my impatience before again seeking her love. I thought it strange that no answer came to my letter. Mr. Austin, too, became anxious, for he had not heard from the Daltons for some time. I resolved to go to Montreal at once, and surprise them with a visit. Mr. Austin showed much regret when I spoke of leaving them. "Something tells me you will not come back," he said; "but wherever you go, I pray that God will bless you"

That night—Sunday it was—I stood in the crowded church listening to his loved voice for the last time. Every word he spoke seemed intended for me alone. It all struck me so forcibly, that I remember it to this day. He took his text from the third chapter of St. John, 36th verse: "He that believeth on the Son hath everlasting life; and he that believeth not the Son shall not see life, but the wrath of God abideth on him." "Those words," he continued, in a reverent tone, "refer to Jesus Christ—Son of the living God—who partook of our human nature, that we might the better understand Him. Had He come as a conquering king, surrounded with majesty and glory, men would have shrunk from Him in terror and affright—even as the Israelites did at Mount Sinai; but behold, He came as a lowly child, sharing all the privations and miseries so common to humanity. Some say He was not God; but, if He was not God, who was He? Surely no false prophet! Surely no ordinary man! He must have been God, or He would not have promised so much. Has He not said, 'I am with you always.' How could He say this if He did not possess the power to be always with us? O ye men of little faith, can you not pierce the clouds of doubt that surround you, and fly onward through the dark sea of misery, and enter in imagination the unknown world, where you can picture Him in the perfection of glory? But if your faith will not do this, then take your Bible and read carefully His earthly life, and find there thy proof, O doubting soul."

Some more words followed, and then, after the usual service, I went alone out into the moonlight, pondering over the words that had impressed me. Once I would have laughed at it all. How often had I ridiculed Christians and called them superstitious fools! but I regretted it now. How much good might have resulted, had I known the truth in my earlier years! No wonder that Alice had shrunk from the idea of marrying me. I was unworthy of her in every way. Perhaps now, if I returned to her, she would receive me coldly; but, if she would not marry me, I would be content to live near her and see her sometimes. Life apart from her would be a living death: yet, once married to her, I could become good and noble. With her to help me I could accomplish great things, without her I was helpless.

A strange sensation came over me as I thought of her. It seemed to me that I was conscious of her presence near me; and I almost fancied that I could hear her voice whispering to me amid the shadows. And then I pictured her as I had seen her last—a pretty figure in the snow-bound scenery—and I wondered greatly how she would receive me. Would it be with glad surprise, or cold displeasure?

I had drawn near to the house and was about to enter, when I was startled by the figure of a man, emerging from the shadow of a tree near by. As viewed in the rays of the fitful moonlight, there was something familiar in the attitude of the form that reminded me of the past.

"Is it you, Arthur?" he said. And as he spoke I recognized him. I was face to face with my father.

"You!" I cried, in amazement, "what brings you here?"

"Come inside," he said, with a sigh, "and I will tell you all."

I was so utterly astonished by his unexpected presence that I complied without a word; and together we entered the house.

"You wonder how I have found you," he began, after we were seated in my own room. "I heard of you in Boston, where you buried that woman you called your wife. From there I traced you here; and I am sorry to see you have fallen so low as this." Here he glanced contemptuously around the plainly-furnished room.

"And yet," I answered, "I am about to begin a life wherein I shall be happier than I have ever been."

"Rubbish!" he retorted; "people make their

own happiness, and spoil it, too, very often. However, I am not here to reproach you with the past. My other children are dead. I am now a childless man, whose years perhaps are numbered; and I am come to offer you back your rightful place in your own home. You have sown your wild oats, and I expect you to settle down now to a quiet life."

"Do you know that I have become a Christain?" I asked, after a slight pause.

"I have judged as much from the people you are living with," he replied, "but you will give up all those foolish ideas. I think you are only acting a part, and don't believe in Christianity any more than I do."

"You are laboring under a mistake," I rejoined, somewhat hastily, "I am not playing a part. My eyes have been opened and I know the truth."

"What nonsense!" he answered; "you will find it is only a mockery—all the creation of some man's brain."

"No," I answered, "it is the truth; and if I comply with your request and return home, it will be with the assurance that I shall have liberty to practice Christianity. Besides, I intend to seek the hand of a Christian lady in marriage."

"You are just as stubborn as ever," he said; "I might as well have remained at home. You have always thwarted every wish of mine."

"I am sorry, but I cannot give up my opinions," I answered, "and there is more happiness for me in the path I have marked out for the future, if I only succeed in winning the woman I love."

He came closer to me, a pleading look softening his features. "My boy," he said, "will you not give up all those ideas and return with me? You will soon forget it all."

"Have I not already answered you?" I replied.

"But you do not mean that," he answered. "Have I not told you that I am childless, and my home is desolate. Return to your old home and forget this woman you speak of. I am your father, and should have the first claim on your affection."

For the moment my heart softened towards him, as I perceived the change sorrow had wrought in his appearance. His once vigorous form looked feeble and bent, and deep lines of care marked his countenance. I was undecided how to answer him. I never thought for an instant of giving up the plan I had formed. Softly through my heart came the remembrance of some words Alice had once said to me: "The man who would renounce all the wealth of the world, forsaking all for Christ—I should deem him worthy of being called a hero."

"I have not very long to live," my father went on; "and at my death you will possess all I have."

"No," I answered, "it can never be; now that I have found the truth, I cannot lightly throw it aside."

"You will repent it one day," he said, in anger, "when this woman turns from you; and then you will wish you had done as I asked you."

He turned as if to leave the room, but I called him back. "Stay," I said. "Before you go I have something to tell you. While I was an atheist I knew no real happiness. You know well all the misery I caused those around me; but as I sinned, so have I suffered. When in an hour of dark despair I intended to kill those who had wronged me—and then myself—there came to me an angel in human form. She was only a Christian maiden with a pure and lofty soul. Daily I lived in her presence and grew to love her, even as the flowers love the sunshine. She it was who brought my soul from the heavy darkness of sin into the eternal light. Don't think it was an easy task, for the strong belief of years was hard to battle with, and even now I have much to learn; still, though unworthy of the name, I call myself a Christian."

"What is the use of telling me all this?" he said in an angry tone. "I tell you that some day you will be sorry for it!"

I followed him out into the hall, loth to part from him in anger. "Is this a final parting?" I asked; "can there be no peace between us?"

"No," he said, sternly. "I was a fool to come near you."

It was with a heavy heart I saw him take his departure, watching his form till it faded from my sight; and so we parted to meet on earth no more.

This visit of his somewhat damped my happiness. I did not like to think of him as miserable in his old age. I comforted myself with the reflection that I would tell Alice all about it. She would advise me what was best to do; and, before retiring to rest, I made the few necessary preparations for my journey.

It was a bright sunshiny morning when I started for Montreal, and my heart beat high in anticipation of happier days. Mr. Austin wrung my hand warmly at parting. "If anything happens to frustrate your plans," he said, "you must return here and make your home with us." I thanked him and promised to do so, yet hoped that it would be otherwise. No foreboding came to me of anything wrong. I believed that fate intended to be kind to me at last, and that the future would be clear and bright.

Is it not a merciful Providence that has ordained it so? Thank your God, O ye people of the earth, that the future is hidden from you in a sea of mystery!! Be happy in the present, well content to leave the future in His hands, and seek not to pry into that which He has intended you should not know; for "sufficient unto the day is the evil thereof." And when life's brief journey is ended, and the spirit world with all its wonders is opened to you, then will you see light on subjects which now seem so dark to you; then will you know the "why" and "wherefore" of "this thing" and "that." So, be comforted, O ye troubled hearts! Know ye, that not even a sparrow falls unnoticed by the Father; and how much more worthy of His regard are ye, O men of little faith!

CHAPTER XIV.

THE WAGES OF SIN.

When I arrived in Montreal, I could hardly restrain my joy at the prospect of seeing Alice. There was every indication of a heavy storm. Overhead the dark clouds hung thick and heavy, and there was that strange stillness in the atmosphere, sure token that the elements would soon be at war.

Passing a florist's, and knowing the passion that Alice had for flowers, I purchased the choicest blossoms I could find. I had them neatly laid on a bed of green moss; and taking them with me, I hurried to reach the house before the storm should overtake me. I knew that it was a good hour to find them at home. I pictured their surprise on seeing me; and I felt that I should soon know my fate.

I was still unworthy of aspiring to the love of one so good, but I fondly hoped that she would help me to attain that perfection which she had already reached. The door was opened by the same girl that was with them when I left. She gave a start of surprise on beholding me.

"Is Mr. Dalton at home?" I asked, as I followed her into the house.

"Why, no," she replied; "did he not write to you before he went to England?"

"I did not hear of it," I said. "Tell Miss Dalton that I am here."

The girl looked at me in astonishment. "Do you not know," she replied, "that Miss Dalton is dead?"

I looked at her in sudden rage. "Don't jest with me," I said impatiently.

"I am in earnest," she answered; "see, here is the notice of her death I cut from the paper. Mr. Dalton was so broken-hearted by the blow that he could not bear to live here."

I gazed around the familiar room and half expected to see her come forward to greet me. I tried to read the notice, but the words seemed to dance before my eyes.

"How did it happen?" I asked, as the awful truth burst upon me.

"It was fever," the girl answered. "Poor, gentle creature, she was visiting some of the poor and found some stricken with disease. It proved contagious; and in a few days she was in her bed, never to rise again."

Here the good-natured girl pressed her hand over her eyes to hide the tears. "It was pitiful, sir," she went on, "to see one so good taken, while the bad ones are left. But she never murmured; she was patient to the end."

"Take me to the room she died in," I said; and in silence I ascended the staircase.

"Here it is, sir," the girl said, opening a door.

"Will you leave me here for a little while?" I asked; "I would rather be alone."

She complied, closing the door after her; and I gazed about me in mute despair. How well I knew that room! How familiar was each object! It was the dainty rose-tinted room in which I had first beheld her. She must have occupied it after I left. My eyes fell on the flowers I had brought for her. I had chosen them, because I knew she would prize them better than the rarest jewels. Now my heart was smitten with anguish, as I realized the truth. I dashed the box on the floor and stamped upon it in my rage. Outside the storm had burst in all its fury, and I crouched by the open window and spread my arms out into the gathering darkness. "Dead!" I cried, "and I knew it not! Dead! and must I still live on? and through the coming years shall I listen in vain for the sound of her dear voice? No, no, she cannot be dead!" "Dead!" The lightning seemed to whisper the word as it flashed upon my stricken form. "Dead!" the thunder echoed as it died away in the distance. "Dead!" cried my despairing heart. "How can she be dead? She believed in another life! She must live on somewhere! Such a soul was not created for this passing life! She must still live on! She was too good to die!" I peered out into the vapory darkness and eagerly scanned the angry sky, as if my eyes could pierce the veil of mystery that hid her from my sight.

"O my darling!" I cried, "can my eyes not reach thee on that unknown shore? Can I not see thy spirit face, or behold thy phantom form? Never, never, till I too am dead!"

Softly through the rising mists I fancied I saw her come. Methought I saw her dear face smiling on me in my anguish; while borne on the rustling wind came the faint sound of her spirit voice. "I am not dead," it seemed to say; "I live again in Christ."

I held out my hands as if to grasp her, but they encountered only the cold rain drops. I called aloud to her, but the thunder drowned my voice, and nothing remained but the empty darkness. She was not dead! O blessed assurance! My darling lived, lived on, glorified and immortal. I bowed my head, and my soul went out in adoration to the God who had blessed us with an immortal life.

I could no longer doubt the immortality of the soul.

"O God of the sorrowful," I prayed, "help me to bear this blow. All my life I have ignored Thee—have despised Thy doctrines. Now, O God, I beseech Thee to let me live the life my darling led. Make me like her, so that I may one day be deemed worthy of living with her in Thy eternal home!"

The thought comforted me, and I arose, resolved to devote my life to Christ as she had done.

"Spirit of my dead Alice, descend upon me!" I cried, "and help me through the dreary years. Give me thy blessing to comfort and cheer me in the lonely future!"

How desolate the future appeared to me! How dreary the coming years! Yet in the distance, hope, like a lone star, shone upon me —the hope of one day entering the immortal life, where I could enjoy the eternal peace with her who was dead to me in life.

Through all my grief I perceived the hand of God heavy against me. I had sinned deeply, and "the wages of sin is death." A living death was my punishment—a life wherein no joy could enter; for with the loss of her I loved came death to every joy of my existence.

To Alice there came no death. It was merely a short journey—a passing transition from a dark world of sin to brighter spheres of eternal peace and joy.

I left the house—a sad and altered man. I was undecided where I should go. I longed to visit my old home, and view once more the scenes of my childhood. Who, in an hour of sorrow, does not remember with regret the happy hours of childhood?

I knew it was useless for me to think of going home—there would only be another quarrel with my father. I knew that we would never agree on the subject of religion, and I thought

I had better return to Mr. Austin. With him I would commence a life of help and devotion to the Master's cause.

The next day found me on my way to him. I was received with looks of surprise at my changed appearance. I had left them a young man, full of hope; and I returned, haggard and prematurely aged—my dark hair plentifully sprinkled with threads of silvery white. I told them what had happened, and the worthy couple were greatly shocked at the sad news.

"But why should we mourn for her?" Mr. Austin said; "we know that she has entered that eternal rest which God gives His beloved."

I told Mr. Austin the life I had intended to lead, and he was much pleased at my decision. "You should study for the ministry," he said, "and when my hour comes to die, I shall rest content that you will faithfully continue the work I have begun."

I promised him I would; but I knew that I would need much improvement before I should be worthy to work as he did.

I wrote to my father and explained to him the disappointment I had received, and also the life I was about to begin. I received no answer for some time. Then came a letter from the family lawyer, informing me that my father and his wife were gone to England. Enclosed I found a cheque. It was for a comparatively small amount, yet to me it was very acceptable.

All through the long summer months I studied harder than ever. Mr. Austin was failing fast, and each day found him more feeble, and the hardest work devolved on me. Besides a class for young men, I had Sunday school for the small boys of the village, and the aged poor to attend to; so that my time was fully occupied. Through it all the memory of Alice cheered me on. I knew that I had much to learn before I became the Christian she was; and much to atone for, before I should be worthy to stand in the presence of the incomprehensible God, who was well aware of the faults of the creature He had made. Often in the night I suffered untold pangs of misery; and I lifted my voice to God in the darkness, pleading for mercy and pardon for the past.

Sometimes Mr. Austin would ask me to preach or lecture to the class, and a sense of my unworthiness would come over me. I would be at a loss what to say; but, after a silent prayer, the words would flow, and almost unconsciously I worked upon the feelings of my hearers, until many doubting hearts were convinced.

I did not set myself up amongst them as an example, or a shining light, but as a struggling sinner working for the truth ; and, strange to say, my work was successful, and I accomplished much good. I helped many a despairing fellow-creature into a better way of living ; and many a night, while Mr. Austin took his rest, I went about among the sick and suffering.

Sometimes, when alone with nature, my soul would rise in adoration to God, until by degrees my thoughts were rapt above the earth, away far into the mysterious regions where I knew that Alice dwelt ; and I would try to picture her blest and immortal, reaping the harvest of the good seed she had sown on earth.

It grieved me to think of my father. He never wrote to me ; yet I prayed daily for his conversion, and longed for him to experience the comfort of religion. He was dragging out his existence in darkness and sin, and he would know nothing of eternal life until his soul, bereft of its earthly covering, should stand in the presence of a judging—yet I trusted a merciful —God.

The people around me seemed much affected by my teachings. I did not preach to them after the usual manner. I left aside the doctrines I thought to be mistakes. About eternal punishment, I still had my doubts. I simply urged them to live a life of good. To those who needed help I spoke of the Saviour's love, and of the mercy shown by Him to sinners. At the end of these meetings I would find many waiting to ask me questions, which I sometimes found hard to answer.

"Do you think all sinners will be saved?" one man asked me.

"Look around you," I replied, "and behold the many instances of God's love for sinners. Is it likely that He who cares for us in a life of sin will abandon us in that life in which we hope for rest and reward for our work?"

"But what of the sinners who die without repenting?" the man persisted.

"I think we can trust that God has provided a place of repentance in the life to come. I think it is wrong for us to judge what shall be the future of sinners. He who created them did not do so with the intention of placing them in everlasting torment."

About this time an event took place which threw a gloom over the village—Mr. Austin's death. Poor man, he stood bravely to his post; yet, when death came, he was ready for its summons.

In him I had found a true friend, and I missed him in many ways. A work that he had begun was left to me to finish. Though he was dead his work lived on, and many Christian hearts followed after his example. A younger man replaced him—a man worthy of following in his footsteps.

I took up my head-quarters in the village, and went steadily on with my work. I left myself completely in the hands of God. Sometimes I would wander away from home, wherever His spirit led me, and preach the Gospel. In this way the years passed, and I waited patiently till death should set my spirit free to rest from my labors.

I shall now pass over a longer period of such a life—some ten years or more—and again I will come before the reader, as an old man—a man whose days are numbered, and whose heart was buried in the grave of the woman he loved. Yet I would speak a word of warning before closing these earthly scenes. I would ask you people of the earth so to live, that when you die you can look back on life without a shudder for your crimes. Here, everything is so pure, so calm, so peaceful, that the sins committed on earth rise up and haunt the memory—even as the murderer is haunted by the cries of his victim.

And now I am nearing the end of my history on earth—nearing that scene in which the Angel of Death will play a prominent part. Read it as a message from another world; for it is true, and truth will prevail!

CHAPTER XV.

CLOSING SCENES.

SLOWLY in the western sky the autumn sun is sinking to its rest. All day long it has scorched with its powerful rays each tiny flower and blade of grass that deck the meadows. Now a gentle dew refreshes the parched earth; while a soft wind sweeps gradually over the rising landscape. I stand alone on the hillside and gaze around me. Beneath lay the village—the scene of my labors. Why was I loth to leave it, I wondered; for in my hand I held a letter that called me thence, and the prospect saddened me. But I knew it was my duty, and I would go. The letter was from Boston, urging me to come at once and begin my labors there. Never did the village seem so dear to me as when I knew I must leave it. Still my work there was nearly ended. I should leave behind me many true Christians, many true soldiers of God. Across the meadows came the laborers, returning from their day's work. They greeted me kindly as they passed. How well I knew them all! Not one that had not come to me and told me his hopes and joys. It would be hard to say farewell, hard to leave them, perhaps for ever. Yet I would not hesitate to obey duty's call. Go, I must, be the results good or evil; and I trusted that He whose hand had led me thus far would lead me safely to the end. Soon the villagers had all passed, and I was again alone, though in the distance I could discern their forms as they loitered on the way, resting from the labors of the day.

A stranger passing through the village would behold those scenes as in days of yore—the merry children playing in their childish glee, the solitary couple loitering in the by-ways; all peaceful and calm, watched over by the Father with loving care.

As I walked homeward in the gathering twilight, recollections of by-gone years stole over me. Again I fancied myself a youth standing on the threshold of manhood, the future looming bright and clear before me. And then, the faces of loved ones floated through my fancy. Lastly, I wondered if, when my earthly probation was ended, I should find those who had gone before.

I had never been gifted with poetical fancies, but now my life came rhyming in verses through my brain. I give them as they were—called

THE STREAM OF LIFE.

I was floating down the river—
    The river called the Stream of Life—
Knowing not of God, the Giver
    Of the bright, eternal Life.

Then the Stream of Life grew troubled;
    Darkness hid me from the shore;
"I am lost!" I vainly shouted;
    "I am lost for evermore!"

And the angry waters near me—
    The waters called the Sea of Death—
Were ever ready to engulf me
    'Neath their dark and dismal depth.

But the Father, ever watchful
    Of the precious soul He'd made,
Led my Spirit, weak and doubtful,
    To the shore, 'neath mercy's shade.

There the darkness faded from me,
    I had found the truth at last,
And th' eternal light shone on me;
    I was saved—the danger past.

Gently then the stream flowed onward;
    I floated on without a care,
Steering my frail craft homeward,
    Safe beneath the Father's care.

Now Life's Stream is nearly ended;
    Soon I'll reach the eternal shore,
Where, in joy and glory blended,
    I hope to reign for ever more.

I wrote the words on a slip of paper, which I afterwards lost; but they are fresh in my memory still.

It was no easy task to inform the simple-hearted villagers of my intended departure. They had become attached to me, and I to them. They had made me a sharer of their joys and sorrows; and many were the looks of regret when they heard that I was going to leave them.

Once I had made up my mind, I did not linger long, but began preparations to start without delay. The night before my journey I entered the class-room to say a few parting words. They were all there—the people I had worked amongst. The room was crowded—many with sad faces and dejected air. How vividly they rise before me now—those faces of the past! Some of them I meet here; and oh! how happy is that meeting, where there is no earthly care to mar the joy, no dark clouds to dim the future! It is but the answer to my prayer of that night; for, as we knelt in prayer, I besought the God of Glory, who had ordained that we should part, that in His own time we should meet together in the glory of His immortal home. It was over at last: the final good-bye spoken, the last farewell whispered, accompanied by hearty hand-shakes and many wishes of God-speed; and I lingered in the doorway—a lonely figure—as I watched them fading from sight, little knowing that it was the last I should see of them on earth.

The next morning I started early for the scene of my new work. Boston was much the same then as it is now. I had plenty of work to do: I found many sinful souls; and I did my utmost to save them from a life of crime.

About this time it entered my head to write the history of my life and publish it to the world, thinking it would perhaps prove a lesson to mankind; but I had not much time to begin it, so I determined to wait until I could obtain time to go to Montreal. There, where I had found salvation, I would write a full account of it. My father was still in England, and strangers occupied the old home. I did not go there—old memories were too strong within me just then; so I contented myself with my work, well satisfied that I was doing some good; and God looked on my efforts and blessed them, and my work prospered.

In midwinter I suddenly made up my mind to visit Montreal, where there was to be a Carnival.* The rates would be reduced, and, as my means were limited, I concluded to avail myself of the chance. Once there, I would take some rest, and then begin my history.

Strange that I fancied Alice so near me at that time. It seemed to me that she was directing me onward. I had never forgotten a single expression of her dear face; it was as fresh in my memory as the first time I beheld her. Other faces, fair and beautiful, had crossed my path, but never one with such an expression of purity and truth as hers. It would pain me, I knew, to visit the old scenes wherein I had first known her; but I would conquer my sorrow, trusting that some day it would pass away and in the end I should know peace.

I purchased a return ticket on the Central Vermont line, and, without telling any one where I was going, I started on my journey. I had a reason for secrecy: many Bostonians would be in Montreal, and, if they knew I was there, would expect me to join them; but I was going, not for amusement, but for rest.

---

*The Carnival of 1887.

The night was clear and frosty. From above a bright moon sent down her silvery rays, causing the leafless trees to cast their shadows on the snow-bound region. On, on, the engine rushed, with its train of cars, scattering in every direction a shower of fiery sparks. On, on, it went, speeding past the quaint homesteads and quiet villages that looked so weird in the moonlight.

There was the usual rumbling noise. Many of the passengers had retired to rest, sleeping all unconscious of the cruel fate so soon to overtake them. I was sitting alone, reading an extract from a sermon I had copied. The air of the car was insufferably close. The stoves were filled with burning coals that sent forth an intense heat, making the hot air flutter through the car like faint smoke. There came to me no thought of danger—all was so tranquil. I sat there, calm, and knowing not that I should not see, in life, the well-remembered scenes I was then looking forward to.

There was a screech from the locomotive as it neared a small wooden bridge. Suddenly I felt a swerving, jolting motion; there was a crash, and before I realized what had happened,

I felt myself falling through space, the broken timbers falling around me, while shouts of wild horror arose on the frosty air. I came in contact with the cold ground, and then became oblivious of all around me.

I must have sunk into a dream or trance. It seemed as if I stood in the midst of a fragrant garden, where many rare things passed before my wondering eyes. Bright-plumaged birds filled the air with their sweet song, and all around me flowers of rich variety sprang in their verdant beauty. A stream of crystal water flowed beside me, and on the brink stood a woman clad in robes of white. Slowly she turned towards me and I beheld the face of Alice. I tried to reach her, but some unseen force held me back. All the passionate love arose within me. Ah, if I could only reach her, I would never let her from my grasp! Death itself would not possess the power to sever us! If she would but come closer, I would tell her that, living or dead, she was mine!

It turned dark, and the bright dream was gone. I awoke to the awful reality. The sky above me was lit up with a lurid glare, and I could hear the fierce roaring of the flames as they went on with their deadly work.

For five or ten minutes I lay trying to recall what had happened. I tried to rise, but I was covered with the fallen *debris* and broken timber, and found that I could not stir. I felt as if I was freezing, yet ever nearer to me came the deadly flames, while the cries, and appeals for help which could not be rendered, were perfectly frightful to listen to.

Suddenly I awoke to a sense of my own danger. Unless help soon reached me I was doomed. I gazed around me helplessly. Nearer came the flames; already I could feel their hot breath. Yes, God help me, I thought, I was doomed to an awful death. In that minute every act of my life arose before me with startling distinctness. Faces that I had forgotten—the old, evil companions of the gambling den—now came before me, mocking my anguish. All Christians believe in a hell; but there is no hell with half the terrors of a dying guilty conscience. Oh the deep agony of the moment, when the foreboding anguish thrilled my soul that death was near me! A horrible darkness overshadowed my soul, and I seemed lost in a sea of night. Intense pain racked my body, but the agony of my mind was greater. The time must have been very short, but to me it seemed ages, all my sins rising before me like demons of darkness torturing my soul ere its flight. In my mind there was no remembrance of the good I had done; only the evil haunted me. Strange, too, that I did not think of Alice! It was my mother I thought of in my last agony. I seemed to see her smiling on me from a place of light, but hell-hounds seemed to drag me from her into outer darkness, where there was wailing and weeping and gnashing of teeth.

Could this be hell? I asked myself; and was I doomed to suffer the torments of the damned? All the people I had ever wronged came to haunt me in my agony, their cries making it all the more hideous. Deeper, deeper grew the darkness; thicker, thicker grew the mist; loud voices shouted around me, till my spirit felt faint with terror.

Was this eternal life—this awful anguish? Was this the life I had been looking forward to? Where was the Christ who had promised to save sinners? Where was Alice? Surely my love was strong enough to draw her to me!

"O Christ!" I prayed, "have mercy on me; into Thy hands I commend my spirit."

As I said the words, the terror vanished: the darkness gradually disappeared, and I seemed to see the face of Christ beaming on me.

A loud noise startled me back to life. The timbers of the bridge had given way, falling on the struggling mass of wounded people, dealing death and destruction all around. Something heavy struck me; and, with one last thrill of mortal agony I was numbered with the dead.*

For a long time after, I seemed lying in a sleep. My first sensation was like that of a tired man, awakened from a deep sleep. My spirit was weary with the struggle it had undergone, and was quietly gaining strength. I found myself reclining on what appeared to be a fleecy cloud.

All seemed natural to me. I did not feel at all strange, though apparently suspended between heaven and earth. Other inhabitants of the air were floating around me, and I found that I could float any distance at will. From beneath me, I could see a long, long distance. The world looked very small to me, and I began floating downward to view it closer.

---

* The appalling accident, here so vividly described, which occurred at White River Junction early in the morning of the 5th February, 1887, must be fresh in the recollection of every-one.

When my spirit passed away, it must have floated, or been carried, to the cloud whereon I rested, where it must have lain dormant; for, as I approached the earth, I found the sun had already risen.

The first thing that greeted my vision was the scene of the accident; other spirits were crowding around, and I mingled with them. I now saw that it had been caused by a broken rail. The rear sleeper had fallen over the embankment, carrying with it the passenger coaches, containing upwards of eighty-four persons. Many of them told me, in the spirit-world, that they had died before reaching the bottom of the embankment. A bystander remarked that the time from the accident to the falling of the bridge was about fifteen minutes. This was the time of my agony; but how long it had seemed to me! Even then I could not recall it without a shudder.

I looked for some trace of my mangled body, but it was not visible; it was no doubt charred and disfigured beyond recognition. It was not very comforting to reflect on. My friends would not know what had become of me; and my father would not even know that I was dead.

As I thought of this, I determined to go and try to make known to him that I had passed from earth. I accordingly began ascending from the dreary scene of death, and I floated with quick motion over land and sea. It was delightful—this easy floating through space. I would not wish for any other existence; yet, at the same time, I wondered where heaven was. Strange too, that I no longer longed for Alice! All earthly passions had vanished. I felt all-sufficient in myself. Numbers of spirits, in bands, passed me, all seemingly intent on some mission. Now and then I beheld a solitary form like my own. I reached England. I found that my father lived in the West. I had nothing to guide me save instinct, which is very powerful in spirit life. I found that I had power to inspect the dwellings over which I passed. All spirits do not possess this power. Many acquire it after long years, but I found that I possessed it from the first.

And people called this death! To me it was a life of bliss. So, farewell, all earthly labour! farewell, all earthly care! never more will you annoy me; yet from the height of Brighter Spheres will I view your progress, O world!

Though you look so small and insignificant from where I am, still I remember that I once mingled in your scenes—once shared your sorrows and your joys. Now, O world! I look calmly back to that time and say :

"'O death, where is thy sting? O grave, where is thy victory?'"

CHAPTER XVI.

THE SPIRIT WORLD.

It was night on the shores of England—a clear, still night. I found my father's house—a rich mansion, a-blaze with lights and crowded with guests. Mrs. Rogers was evidently holding a reception. I looked in vain for my father in the crowded rooms. He was not there, but something drew me onward to the conservatory at the rear of the house. There, seated on a low seat, shaded by the large tropical plants, was my father—alone and cheerless-looking. He appeared to have fallen into a light slumber; and as I drew nearer, I perceived that he was watched over by the spirit of a woman—a being with a pure and beaming countenance—who gently stroked his care-worn face. I wondered that he could not feel that touch; once he stirred uneasily in his slumber—he was dreaming.

I felt strangely attracted by the face of the woman, who looked so tender in her loving care. She raised her head, and our eyes met in one fond glance of recognition. Oh, the unutterable joy of the moment, when, in spirit life, I first beheld my mother! She knew me at once; the change of years cannot hide a child from a mother's heart. "My boy!" she said, "I have been waiting for you here; I knew that you would come."

"Now," I said, " I understand what instinct drew me here; you were waiting for me."

"Yes," she answered; "but come, let us go hence. Your father sleeps."

"Poor man!" I said, "he does not look happy."

"Come closer," she said, "and read his thoughts."

I placed my head close to his, and found that I could distinctly read his very thoughts; he was dreaming of his youth.

"We will come back to him again," my mother said. "You have yet to view the wonders of this life."

"But where is heaven, mother?" I asked her, as together we floated upwards.

"Heaven, my son," she answered, " is so vast, so beautiful, so grand, it will take you a long time to reach it."

We travelled a great distance upwards, far beyond the "limits of space." The air around us seemed to grow radiant with light, while strains of sweet music were wafted from the distance. Spirits with beaming faces smiled on us as they passed.

I felt strangely happy: my spirit seemed animated with fresh energy: I retained all my mental faculties, and my memory was much clearer than it had ever been. We reached a place that seemed made of golden clouds; it was from this place that the music floated. Spirit forms were hovering near, as if anxious to enter this place of light; some tried to enter, but were sent back.

"How is this?" I asked my mother. "Why are they sent back?"

"They are not good enough," she answered. "This is a high sphere where only those who have done penance for their sins can enter. All are pure and spotless who dwell therein."

"This is not heaven, then?" I queried.

"No," she said, "what is called heaven, is the highest sphere of all. You will have to go through many before you are considered worthy to enter it; for there is found the perfection of spirit life."

"But how can they tell here," I asked, "whether spirits are worthy or not?"

"Oh! my son," she said, "there are pure and noble spirits in charge who are much wiser than we are. They are appointed by God to be the guardian angels of men. They are familiar with our good deeds and our bad. If the bad deeds overbalance the good, we could not enter until the good were in the ascendancy. We are judged, not so much by the bad we have done as by the good; for 'the good tree bringeth forth good fruit.'"

"Then a man can atone, in this life, for the crimes committed on earth?"

"Yes," she answered, "there are many ways of atonement, until gradually the stain of guilt disappears and the spirit is pure enough to enter a higher sphere. But follow me, we will go in."

I floated after her into the City of Light, whose radiance dazzled me. It was lighted with numerous suns, whose brilliant rays were reflected on the jasper pavement, and on the buildings, which seemed composed of a substance like marble and gold. We entered a fragrant garden, furnished with shady retreats. It was a pure and peaceful atmosphere, and already my spirit was glorified by the purity of the air around me. Such must be the atmosphere where so many holy beings live immortalized.

I entered a cool retreat and watched them as they passed—those celestial people. They were clothed in garments of white, and their faces shone with holiness and love. I saw the form of a woman advancing towards me. She seemed so pure and holy that other spirits bowed low before her as she passed; because she had descended from a higher sphere.

As she neared me I felt as if I must fall down and worship her—she was so bright and lovely. But she smiled on me, and I recognized her; it was Alice, shining in immortality.

I rushed to greet her, but she drew back: "I am not first; here is one who has long waited for this meeting." I looked and beheld another form, less lovely; it was Maud—my wife—beaming on me with looks of love and forgiveness.

It was a joyful meeting. Earthly mortals have no idea of the bliss experienced in brighter spheres.

We conversed together for a long time. Other friends crowded around to welcome me, among whom were Mr. Austin and other friends of my village home. Here, too, I met relatives I had never known. Here the bond of relationship is strong; all love each other—rank makes no distinction.

"We will leave you now," my mother said, "you need some rest."

"Why must you leave me so soon?" I asked.

"We belong to a higher sphere," Maud explained; "you must remember that we are long residents here. After a length of time spent here the spirit becomes very pure. Do you know that from the other spheres we can watch over you, just as from this one you can behold what is passing on earth. Look!

I peered over what seemed a deep cliff or ravine, where vapory clouds ascended, and I could distinctly see the world revolving beneath me like a huge globe, its different countries visible, and a portion of it wholly uninhabited. The other planets were more beautiful than the world I had lived on; they were all inhabited. He who created them had a double purpose in view.

Bands of spirits now came floating upwards from those planets and the earth; some of them with written records of what they had seen—the crimes and sins of men, which were numerous.

"Do you know anything of Rose?" I asked Alice. "It would spoil my joy if I thought she was unhappy."

"No," Alice replied, "she is happy, but she is now atoning for many sinful hours spent on earth. She is called a Spirit of Mercy; and is ever on the earth trying to do good for the sons of men."

My friends now left me, and I rested; for I was somewhat dazed by the wonders I had beheld. It was a world of peace and beauty, where divine grace dwelt undisturbed by sin. The inhabitants were all shining with joy—no sadness or sorrow anywhere.

Other joys awaited me after my rest. I was able to wander at will—sometimes in company with Maud or Alice—through the other planets, whose beauty amazed me.

In this way some months must have passed, but to me they were like so many hours. The years here are like days. As yet I have not beheld half the glory of God's dominions; for "in the Father's house are many mansions." He dwells in the highest heavens, and rules the spirit world. Only the purest and holiest spirits dwell in His presence. These seldom visit the earth—only on some particular mission. When God commands, they obey.

'There are many kinds of spirits. Some are Spirits of Mercy sent by God to the earth to relieve the over-burdened sinner when he cries for divine help. Then, there are Spirits of Love and Charity direct from God, filling the hearts of the righteous with love for their fellow-creatures, and eternal love for the Father of Mercies.

The Spirits of Purity hover around the young and innocent, protecting them from the evil spirits that are ever on the earth.

There are also Spirits of Hope, who descend on earth to cheer the despairing sinner, and whisper to him of the eternal life awaiting him.

The Spirits of Faith hover in the churches, softly breathing of the divine love that never fails.

Spirits of Grace are ever with the good. I have seen a minister preaching under the control of seven spirits, each whispering a heavenly thought.

When a man commits a great crime, good spirits forsake him. They are not allowed to associate too closely with evil—except Spirits of Mercy, who are ever striving to bring the sinner to repentance.

There are also Spirits of Death, whose task is very hard. If a good man commits a crime and dies in a state of sin, he first goes through a certain amount of punishment; then he is made a Spirit of Death until such time as he is pure enough to enter a higher sphere. Their name is legion—those Spirits of Death—each working a mission.

Spirits often go in bands: thus Love accompanies Charity; Mercy, Hope; Faith and Peace go with Death. All is order and spiritual law. Millions upon millions have their different missions. There are many without a mission— good people, such as Alice, who rest and reap their reward; for their work was good on earth.

A wealthy man, who has lived a life of ease may be a member of a church, and call himself a Christian, but that alone does not please God; He wants His servants to work in His canse.

If it is not done on earth, they will have to work in spirit life. How much better then it would be to accomplish good on earth! God does not create a soul without a purpose; He marks out for each a mission, which, if not fulfilled on earth, must be done here!

There are many here who have occupied a lofty station in life, caring naught for their fellow-creatures; yet now they go about, unseen, among the poverty-stricken on earth, helping them, putting thoughts into their minds of how to win eternal life. Sometimes men listen to these spirit voices and do not obey. This is wrong. If some instinct warns you to do a good deed, be sure a good spirit is near you. Life is sometimes saved in this way. God is not ready to claim it, and sends a spirit who whispers "do this, or that;" and by obeying, you will soon find that if you had done otherwise something serious would have happened.

There are Guardian Spirits, or Angels, more commonly called. When a child is born the pure spirit of a child is taught to watch over it, and as the child grows, the spirit expands and guides it to the end. Yet Guardian Angels are not always on earth. They remain for long periods in brighter spheres, but they send Spirits of Love, Mercy, Hope and Peace to those they guard. Sin and crime displease these Spirits, because it displeases God.

Sin is always punished—to what extent I am not at liberty to say. Some day you will know all. That which seems so incomprehensible now will all be understood, when, through the portals of death, you enter brighter spheres.

When sinners are heavily punished with deep afflictions on earth, their sufferings are lessened here. O sons of men! could you but know the eternal glory and perpetual joy that here await you, then would you forsake the path of sin and live as you would die, in love and fellowship with each other; for here all is love—earthly passions are no more. A man beholds his mother, wife, sister, but feels they are not necessary to his happiness. We all know and love each other.

If a man of a drunken, quarrelsome disposition dies, he cannot enter the higher spheres until his spirit is purified of all evil qualities; for with us all is peace. It is that "peace which passeth all understanding," and which can never be experienced on earth, for there the angry discord and sinful strife would mar its beauty.

Many spirits are ever near their loved ones on earth; they can become an influence for good or evil, according to the life led on earth.

There are many unhappy spirits who are waiting till the time of pardon—then they may rest in the higher spheres.

A long time ago there lived a lady of rank, who called herself a Christian. She had a large family of sons, for whose sake she became ambitious. She oppressed the poor; she became a very miser for wealth and social honors; she forgot her God and made wealth her idol. Soon there came a dark hour of pain, and Death called; but she rebelled against the divine will, and called God cruel to take her from earth where her treasure was. When her spirit emerged from the mists, she stood at the Pearly Gates—a faltering spirit, awed by the glory around her.

"Why do you linger?" some spirit asked her.

"I do not want heaven," she murmured; "it would not be heaven to me, apart from those I love."

Back she floated to her home, and lingered there—a silent, mournful spectre. Soon another wife took her vacant place; and, in anguish, she beheld her children neglected, and her wealth squandered in a reckless way. As the years passed, her spirit wandered from place to place. Her boys became wild, and were followed by evil spirits. Oh, the anguish of that mother, as she saw her loved ones in sin and crime! This was her punishment; it was a heavy one.

The pitying Saviour saw her misery, and was touched with compassion. He sent bright Spirits of Mercy to bear her to the realms of the blessed. There her wounded soul received peace. In time she became a Spirit of Mercy, and she again descended to earth. Her home was deserted, and her children scattered on the face of the earth. But nothing could hide them from a mother. She sought them out, and gently touched their sinful hearts with thoughts of childhood and mother. She had become so pure, so bright, from her residence in brighter spheres, that all evil spirits fled from before her. Her boys hearkened to her spirit voice, and repentance stole over them. No more they sinned, but, guided by her spirit, they lived to become noble men. Now they enjoy the glory of spirit life, saved by a mother's love. Such things as this are happening every day.

I have told the foregoing to show that sin and crime pain your loved ones who have gone before. Think of that, criminals, when you are inclined to sin. If you have a loved one in the spirit world, be sure that your crime will cause her pain. It is never too late to repent; and when your spirit shall enter this wondrous world, you will see that your reward is great; for it is written: "Eye hath not seen, nor ear heard, neither have entered into the heart of man, the things which God hath prepared for them that love him." 1 Cor. ii. 9.

CHAPTER XVII.

SCENES I BEHOLD.

It is night in a large city, and a cold rain is falling. The autumn winds howl through the barren tree-tops and scatter the withered leaves in all directions. I hover near the poorest part of the city, where angry voices and deep curses reach me, as the night wind bears them heavenward, where they are recorded in the book of life; for not an idle word or thought falls unnoticed.

In a dark, squalid street in this portion of the town there stands a row of dark, dirty houses. It is a place teeming with poverty and vice. Many evil spirits are lurking in the shadows, but I notice several Spirits of Light enter one of those dwellings, and I follow them. I see a scantily furnished room and signs of extreme poverty. A dim light is burning, throwing faint shadows on the narrow walls. Two pale, sickly children are crying around a low old-fashioned bed, on which lies the body of a man, whose pale countenance, marked with death, wears a resigned expression. Closely over him, and drawing every moment nearer, is a Spirit of Death, sent to call him to eternity. Kneeling beside the bed is the figure of a woman, yet young and beautiful; a dark look of grief is now on her face, for it is her husband—the love and support of her life—who is so slowly, but surely, dying. Spirits of Peace and Hope linger beside her, and I watch the scene with deep interest. The silence is broken by the weak voice of the dying man, as his gaze wanders wildly around. "Weep not," he says, "I will soon be free from pain; already the dark waters are closing over me, and I can feel the icy chill of death." Closer the loving wife bends over him, hiding her own sorrows as she clasps his hand.

"Have you any fear?" she asks. "Shall I pray?"

"I have no fear," he replies. "I know not what awaits me; but all my life I have trusted in God, and I can trust Him in death."

Sweetly she bends over him and repeats "The Lord is my Shepherd." Spirits of Mercy and Hope crowd around her and strengthen her soul. A smile of joy crosses the dying man's features. Gently the Spirit of Death breathes on him; and, without a struggle, his spirit comes forth, glorious and immortal. Bright Angels of Light now enter and bear him upwards, through the darkening clouds, to the eternal rest he has won.

I linger with some other spirits beside the lonely watcher, left desolate. There is no loud outcry, no useless grief. She kneels for a while in silent prayer, the white hands crossed meekly over the lonely heart, the head humbly bowed, as she murmurs: "Thy will be done." There is a sob as she clasps her weeping children. "Hush!" she says. "He is not dead—there is no death; he is but gone before."

O loving faith! O gentle soul! thou hast not seen; thou hast no proof of eternal life; but Christ has said: "Blessed are they who believe, yet have not seen."

Kind friends helped the widow and orphans. She never became rich, but she possesses that which wealth cannot buy—a Christian heart, and God's blessing rests with her always.

The dawn is breaking as I float away to the western portion of the city. Lofty mansions now greet my view—houses of splendor and wealth. I enter one of those wealthy mansions. I behold a room—a perfect bower of beauty—filled with all that money can buy; but no bright spirits hover near—only one Guardian Angel, and she looks weary and sad. On the soft, tiny bed a little child is dying, a sweet, innocent child such as God loves. But no one has ever taught her of God; she knows nothing of Him and His eternal home, for her parents are atheists. She shrinks appalled from the touch of death; she has never heard that there is anything beyond the grave, and to her childish mind all is dark and cruel.

Lovingly the Guardian Angel encircles her, keeping back the evil spirits who are in the room.

"She is mine," called out a Spirit of Darkness, as it tried to reach her.

"Begone!" the Guardian Angel replied; "if she has sinned, on her parent's head rests the blame; for Christ has said: 'Suffer little children to come unto Me.'"

The evil spirit drew back, conquered, and a Spirit of Love floated, radiant, before the child.

"Mamma," she cried, "what is that? I see something all light, and it looks lovely."

"It is nothing," the mother replied; "there is no one here but your father."

"Tell him to hold me," the child pleaded; "I am afraid to die."

The father raises her in his arms. "You will soon fall asleep," he said, "and forget your pain."

"But I am not sleepy—the room is full of light," she answered faintly, "and I hear nice music. Who are those people in white, with such lovely faces? Will they take me with them?"

"They are fancies, my child," the father answered; "you have been dreaming."

"No, no, papa, perhaps they are the angels nurse was speaking about."

"There are no angels, my child," the father said; and, as he spoke, her face grew dark with fear.

"Oh!" she sobbed, "if there were angels I should not be afraid; it would not seem so dark and cold, and they would take care of me."

In vain the heart-broken parents tried to ease her dying hour. They could not comfort her as to the future, for they did not believe in any; yet childish instinct whispered to their darling of another life.

"Father, the pain is gone," she murmured, "and a lovely lady is going to take me in her arms."

Her eyes closed and a happy smile lingered on her features. The Angel of Death loosened her spirit, and, with a glad cry, I beheld her, smiling in her innocence, as she floated past me to a Sphere of Light.

"She sleeps," the mother said; but the father knows that she is dead, and gently lays her down.

A costly funeral is provided, and the frail, golden-haired darling is thought of as no more. They can never picture her in her heavenly home; never know that she sometimes stands in their very midst, laying her tiny hands on their darkened hearts—for she would tell them of the glory of her ever-wondering life, where there is no more sin or death.

How many people there are who will not believe in a future existence! Nothing will convince them. Look around you, O doubting soul, and see that nothing ever dies! The flowers that fade to-day will blossom out again in spring time. The leaves that wither and die will soon be replaced by fresh ones. And so it is with the soul: the outward covering will fade and die, but the soul itself lives on in a brighter life.

Man is not judged by his religion. There are many Christians who profess to serve God, yet, when they enter the Spirit World, they find they have done nothing for Him. Those who would be nearest God in the Spirit World must be nearest Him on earth. They must follow in the footsteps of His Son, Christ—humble, meek, patient Christ—who chose for His friends poor, humble fishermen.

Christians, be not proud; think not yourselves one above the other; but love your neighbor, however bad, however lost! Remember only that a soul exists which God loves. Above all be practical Christians. In days of old, Christ said, "Feed my sheep, feed my lambs;" and there are many of His flock in the by-ways and hedges of life, waiting for help. There is work for those willing; and inasmuch as they do it for one of the least of Christ's brethren, they will have done it unto Him.

Every day I see many instances of man's

inhumanity to man. This defect in human nature helps to darken man's existence. I have seen a man break a woman's heart, and bring a parent's grey hairs in sorrow to the grave; yet he was received in the best society. But let a man practice Christianity, and the world sneers. Blessed are you when men revile you for Christ's sake, for your reward is at hand!

One dark night I went with Alice on her visiting the earth in answer to some appeal for help. We entered the poor district of a large city.

"Where are you going?" I asked her, awed by the look of glory on her countenance.

"I am going on the Master's service," she answered. We floated into a humble dwelling. I beheld a tired mother trying to hush the low wailing of a sick child. On a narrow bed lay the sleeping form of a man; while beside him stood a boy, who, I noticed, was trying to conquer temptation.

"I have come to save that boy," Alice whispered. I looked and saw a dark spirit stoop over the boy, who turned impatiently to his mother.

"I can't stand this," he said; "I will find relief, if I have to steal."

"Hush!" the mother said, "can you not have patience? The Lord will provide."

Again the Spirit of Evil came forward; but this time I noticed that Alice stood between him and the boy, who had moved towards the door.

"Don't be anxious, mother," he said; "since you believe it sinful to steal, for your sake I will beg."

He left the room, and we followed. "Come," said Alice, "I have another scene to show you." We entered the fashionable part of the city, and floated into a lofty mansion. Here I saw about twenty ladies and gentlemen, who were evidently holding a meeting of some sort. One gentleman was quoting Scripture, and another was writing a subscription list for some donation; and I noticed that many of them signed for large sums of money, as their names would be sure to figure in the next day's paper. The meeting then broke up. Alice called me with her, and we followed a party of them towards their wealthy homes. On the corner of a public street stood the boy whose troubles had interested me. Now, I thought, he will find help, these people are charitable and will assist him.

The first couple passed on without seeming to hear him; but the others paused to listen to his sad tale, and one lady drew out her well-filled purse.

"Stop!" said the man who had been quoting Scripture, "I would like to investigate this matter; there are so many of this class of people in the city. See here, my boy!" he added, "to-morrow I will find out if your tale is true; if so, we will help you." And they passed on, while the boy gave a weary sigh as he murmured, "to-morrow may be too late."

At that moment there came along an aged man and a young girl; they were poorly clad, and appeared to be humble people. The girl paused as she saw the boy in his lonely attitude.

"What is wrong?" she asked; "are you in trouble?"

"Yes," replied a street urchin, who had overheard the boy's story; "his pa is sick, and they have no money to buy food."

"Poor little fellow!" she said compassionately. "See, grandpa!" she said to her companion, "I will do without my new dress, and give the money to this boy."

The grandfather made no reply, but gave her his purse.

"Here, little boy!" she said, "this is all the money I have. If you tell me where you live, I will go to-morrow and see your mother."

He took the proffered money, with tears of gratitude, and the donor went smilingly on her way.

"See," said Alice, "that is charity! The first party were members of a leading church. They give largely where their names will be published to the world; but that girl goes to her humble home, glad that she has done good. The world may never know of it; but God has seen the act, and in after years it shall be returned unto her in many ways."

"Give, and it shall be given unto you; good measure, pressed down, and shaken together, and running over, shall men give into your bosom. For with the same measure that ye mete withal it shall be measured to you again."
—St. Luke vi. 38.

CHAPTER XVIII.

MY MISSION.

I AM standing in a garden of Paradise. It is a lovely spot, such as Eden must have been; only here no sin can enter to mar its peace and beauty. From above me the bright-hued radiance of a celestial sun is beaming on the scene of glory. Strains of heavenly music are wafted to me on the perfumed air, and I behold bright-robed messengers, as they descend earthward with direct blessings from the higher spheres. In my hand is a parchment, containing a written command as follows:—

"GO FORTH, O SOUL OF PURITY AND PEACE: DESCEND TO THAT SIN-BOUND REGION CALLED EARTH, AND SEEK OUT ATHEISTS AND UNBELIEVERS, AND ALL WHO BELIEVE NOT IN ETERNAL LIFE, AND WHISPER TO THEM OF GOD AND LOVE. PERCHANCE THEY WILL LISTEN TO THY SPIRIT VOICE. THOU HAST DWELT IN

THE REGIONS OF THE BLESSED, AND DIDST PARTAKE OF THEIR GLORY. MAY ITS RADIANCE FOLLOW THEE! AND HE WHO MADE THY SOUL WILL BLESS THEE WITH SUCCESS."

I folded the parchment, and, leaving my heavenly home, floated towards the scene of my mission.

While I lived on earth, I had known many Atheists, but now I found they were more numerous than I imagined. How could I reach their darkened souls? They were a great cause of sadness in Brighter Spheres. God is so great and good that the very doubt of His existence is the cause of pain to those wiser, who behold the dull, joyless lives of Atheists. I, who had been an unbeliever, could pity them.

I have hovered in the tents of the savage, amid the wilds of the forest: I have wandered among the wilds of Africa; but I have seen none so worthy of pity as he who, notwithstanding modern education and mental culture, can say "There is no God."

I drew near to America—my native land—and brooded over it in silence. It was flourishing and improving, yet everywhere were sin and evil; and my spirit grew sad as I thought of my mission.

"O city of my birth!" I cried, "can I not save thee? Shall I wander amid the old scenes, unnoticed? Shall I stand in your very midst, O people, and you see me not? In vain shall I proclaim to you there is a God—you cannot hear me; and if perchance I lay my spirit hands upon your sin-stained hearts, you will not feel their touch!"

As I stood there, sadly musing, Alice joined me, and I told her of my mission.

"You think it hard," she answered, "but others will help you; and I fondly hope that you will do some good."

At that moment the spirit-form of a woman stood beside us. She was very beautiful, and I looked at her in wonder as she smiled on me.

"Don't you know her?" Alice asked. "It is Rose!" And so it was—more beautiful than in life—more lovely than I had ever known her. A pure, holy look softened her face; no trace remained of earthly passions. So changed was she that I should not have known her.

"Come," she said, "I will help you; together, we will work some good."

And so I began my mission. I hovered in the home of the unbeliever: I attended meetings held by Atheists; and those men in their darkened souls felt an influence for good which they could not explain. But, alas! it did not last long. Worldly cares and evil spirits soon banished all recollection of the good.

"It is all in vain," I thought; "I can never accomplish any good."

One dark, wet night I lingered in a crowded city, seeking those who needed help. Evil spirits were on the alert, and crime, poverty and vice were all around.

"I wonder why it is," I thought, "that those evil spirits are so powerful!"

They are all the souls of those who have led bad lives; those who, when on earth, were possessed of an evil nature—a nature that changed not, nor repented. Death may have appalled, but not changed it. He who lives a life of crime, with no desire to change it, passes into the spirit-world retaining all his evil propensities. Here a chance of repentance is held out to save him, but he will not accept it; he is content rather to wander on the earth, leading better men astray. Sometimes the spirits of good succeed in leading some of these evil ones to a better life.

Wandering through the city, I beheld many scenes of crime, many wretched lives. You who dwell in wealth have no conception of the misery among the poverty-stricken inhabitants of a vast city—and where there is so much misery, crime easily steps in; yet a kindly-spoken word, a helping hand, might arrest it. "Cast thy bread upon the waters, and it shall return to thee after many days."

Nor is charity to the poor the only way. There are many of the rich in need of charity—charity to be patient with their faults, charity not to envy them. This is the hardest charity. It is very easy for a rich man to help a poor man; but the poor man will find it hard to have charity for the rich.

While wandering through the streets in company with Rose, I felt suddenly drawn towards the outskirts of the city. I followed instinct, and came to a deserted-looking house—a place such as people call haunted. I entered the dwelling with Rose, and beheld a number of people seated around a small table. There were many spirits in the room, and they seemed hovering around the table. I noticed one laying his hands on it and it, moved in obedience to his will.

"What does this mean?" I said to Rose. "What are they doing?"

"They are spiritualists," she answered. "See! that boy is the medium. Draw closer and see if you can understand the movement."

I did so, and saw that in some way the boy's soul was responsive to those spirits, and they gently gained power from him to move the table; and when he left the room they went with him. This, I thought, would be a good process for communicating with the sons of men.

Every day after this I visited that house, but found that, though the process would suit me, I could not control the table. There was nothing responsive in those people. Besides, they were merely trying to gain information; they looked upon the movement as a species of fortune-telling. The consequence was that the spirits were of an inferior order, and the communications inferior.

"This will never do," I thought. "I cannot speak my commands to these people; they would not regard them in a proper light."

I determined to wait until such time as I should find the right people to receive my work; for, I thought, in this way I might perhaps carry out my mission. If I could only publish my history to the world, people would see the mistakes so often made. I talked it over with Alice, and she agreed with me.

"Much good may result," she said, "if people only know of this science."

"I will investigate it," I said; "it must be quite unknown as yet. I will endeavor to find out the theory of the movement. Many grand things may be the result."

I first spoke about it to other spirits, and found that many of them were familiar with the process. It has existed since the beginning of the world, but is only now coming into practice. In olden days spirits frequently appeared, and were seen. What happened then could surely happen now, if God willed it. Indeed, spirits sometimes appear at the scene of death—especially in cases of murder or suicide; or, they are sometimes permitted to appear in warning of some calamity. A man once told me that during his life he held many conversations, through this movement, with loved ones gone before.

I soon left America in the distance and turned towards Canada, thinking that, amid the scenes where I had found Christianity, I should find a a way to fulfil my mission.

It was night in the City of Montreal. A quiet stillness brooded over the land, and a gentle, summer wind moved with a low, sighing sound through the many branches of the trees.

In the suburbs of the city I encountered a band of heavenly-looking spirits. I turned and joined them. In the front of this band was the form of a young girl. She was so bright and fair to look upon, that I knew she had descended from a high sphere.

" Where are you going ? " I asked her.

" To a *séance*," she replied,

"A power draws us." Her manner inspired me with confidence, and I told her of my mission.

" Come with us," she said, " I know some one worthy of your trust, it is my father. For years," she went on to say, " he has studied spiritualism, unmindful of the sneers and censures of the world. He has made it his religion, and I think he of all others is the one for this task." *

---

* Reference is here made to E. J. C., the writer of the Introduction ; and the young girl, " so bright and fair to look upon," is his daughter, who passed away in 1878, at the age of fifteen.

I went with her to the centre of the city. We entered a house, and found a number of persons seated around the small table used for spiritualistic meetings. I waited while one of the band controlled the table. The medium was rather young and inexperienced in the movement, but I found that I could control the table for the purpose I had in view. I asked them to write my history, and this work is the result. I know not how the world will receive it, but I trust that the God who has permitted its production will bless it with success. Many will doubt its truth. Others will regard it as something supernatural; and to them I answer in the words of Christ: "Greater things shall you see;" but the hour is not yet come.

CHAPTER XIX.

THE USE AND ABUSE OF SPIRITUALISM.

MANY people will not understand how this work was produced. Spiritualism is as yet comparatively unknown, though practiced extensively throughout the United States. I regret to say that, where money is the object, fraud is introduced.

A spiritist is one who believes in the return of departed souls to the earth they lived on, and in conversing—by the power of a medium—with them. This is done by a soul-force which links us with humanity. In life one often meets with a person who starts some hidden gift within the soul—a person who draws and attracts till a bond exists between two souls that only death seems to sever. This is a language of the soul. So in the medium we find a soul responsive to our own. No bodily strength is needed, or mind power, as some persons think. It is a force by which we can either control the medium or anything on which he lays his hand. Thus, two or three people sit around a table—one may be a medium; if so, there will be some spirit feel a force flowing from the medium, which will impel and attract him.; then this spirit can utilize the force, and the table becomes obedient to his will. He need not touch the table, but by his will can make it tilt. There are also mediums who possess power to bring the spirit to a materialized form, which can be seen and recognized. These mediums are very rare; they need to be very pure and good, otherwise evil spirits will cluster around.

There is nothing in spiritualism contrary to Christianity. If properly used, it would prove the existence of God, and waft the truth from shore to shore.

Those who practice spiritualism should avoid exercising their will on the table. Where a number of persons are sitting, their united will may cause the table to tilt and stop at the required letters. This is not spiritualism; it is simply using mind over matter. In the true movement the medium remains passive. The spirit need not touch the table; he may be far away from it, but his will causes it to spell out any sentence he may wish to communicate.

A medium is one who possesses a soul of unusual power—a soul-force hard to analyze—a subtle something which acts as a magnet in the spirit world and draws us to the earth. This power never dies; it lives after the spirit leaves the body. This is why spirits go about in bands. The gentle spirit that led me here possessed this power, which explains why I felt so strangely drawn to follow the band who clustered around her.

Much depends on the character of the medium; if of an indifferent disposition, the communication will be of an inferior order; if of an evil disposition, spiritualism becomes dangerous, for then evil spirits will come.

I think that the Church of Rome believes in spiritualism, though unconscious of the fact. We read in the history of their saints of certain apparitions and miracles. I believe that those so-called saints, by the self-sacrifice of their lives, attained mediumistic power.

Those who read the Bible will find many instances of this movement. We read of angels in the tent of Abraham. I think all the prophets possessed this power, which accounts for their visions. Also, we read of other appearances, which can only be attributed to spiritualism. I think it was practiced in olden days; then, it was called magic, or supernatural agency.

The church teaches her children that at the hour of death they are sent direct to a heaven of eternal rest, or to a hell of everlasting torment, according to the lives they have led. This doctrine is pondered on, and thought of, until gradually the mind revolts against it. This accounts for so many Atheists. A man is taught to look upon God as angry and unjust. He is taught that for the sin within him he is doomed; and soon he tells himself that such laws are unjust—no God could have created millions of human souls to doom them forever. "There is no God," he says to himself: this conviction grows upon him, and it may take years to convince him of the truth.

O man, how little is thy faith! how unreasonable thy soul! the God that made thee will not lose thee from His sight. The darkness of sin may obscure thee; clouds of crime may cover thee; but ever watchful is the eye of God, penetrating the mists, and blessing thee in His mercy. If God was presented to the world as He really is, so many would not doubt Him; He would be accepted and trusted, for He is worthy of all trust, worthy of all love.

Many may wonder why Christ did not institute the subject of spiritualism, when on earth; but, as it is not necessary to salvation, and as the world was then in its dark ages, it would not have been understood. Even now it is put to improper use, and used as a species of fortune-telling. This is wrong. God alone holds the key of the future, and His agents are not permitted to reveal it. If through this movement you seek to find out the future, you will surely receive false communications. God alone is omniscient. Spirits are wiser than mortals, yet they do not know everything.

It is a grievous sin to practice fraud in this movement; for it is no light subject to converse with those who have passed the river of death.

Should the spirit of some loved one, materialized, stand in the midst of a family, appearing in all the unspotted purity of his celestial home among the sinful dwellers of the earth, and deliver to them some message of heavenly truth, would man then believe, I wonder? or would he still doubt? Man is such an unreasonable creature; he will not believe anything he cannot understand.

Spiritualism is a divine gift of God, and should not be misused. I would advise many not to practice it, as they are not good enough. They try it for the mere sake of gaining information; and when they fail in this they abuse the movement, and say there is no truth in it. Now, there are many spirits wandering around who have led wicked lives. The evil is not yet purified from their nature; and when they get a chance of conversing with men through this movement, they resort to all kinds of talk, which injures the movement.

To those who do not wish to believe in spiritualism, I would like to say that, if rightly practiced, it would prove a blessing. There is nothing unnatural in it; it only proves St. Paul's words; for he says of the body: "It is sown a natural body; it is raised a spiritual body; there is a natural body, and there is a spiritual body." Not only this, but it proves to man the existence of immortal life.

I do not understand why the Church is so against the movement. The only harm it can do, is to confute the doctrine of eternal punishment, which has never done much good. If a man is forced to do good through fear of hell, instead of with the idea of pleasing God, he makes a very poor Christian.

Many will wonder at my contradiction of a doctrine founded on the words of Christ—so deeply misunderstood. Those who wish to investigate the truth will find the words are wrongly translated. There is punishment for sin in the burning flames of a guilty conscience. When a man looks back to earth and beholds his descendants suffering for the sins he has committed, how deep is the anguish that thrills his mind—the innocent children made to bear the burden of another's sin; for the sins of the father are visited on the children, unto the third and fourth generation!

Those who practice spiritualism should do so in all harmony and peace, for the least discord jars on the sensitive soul of the medium, and weakens the force that draws us. Let united love and harmony prevail, and the result will be a bond of unity which draws us closer to humanity.

To those who do not believe in the movement I say: "Seek and you shall find for yourself the truth." There is too much dissension on earth for the truth to spread to many different sects and creeds.

There are many who do not believe in the Divinity of Christ. To those I say, HE IS DIVINE. He is the purest, holiest spirit, after God, and dwells with Him in the highest heavens. I PROCLAIM IT IN A VOICE FROM THE UNSEEN WORLD. He was "perfect God and perfect man; of a reasonable soul and human flesh subsisting; and as the soul and flesh were one man, so God and man are one Christ." Those who say otherwise have much to learn.

And the very Christ, despised on earth, is the one we look to in spirit life. We hear His voice speaking to those who have completed their mission: " Enter, ye blessed, into the Kingdom of my Father."

As for those who will not believe in Thee, O patient Christ, fain would I echo thy sorrowful words: " Father, forgive them, for they know not what they do."

CHAPTER XX.

THE END.

MANY people have a theory that at the hour of death they enter a place called heaven. Now this heaven is supposed to exist beyond the clouds, where golden harps and sweet music fill the air with strains of melody; and, once the soul enters, there it remains for ever.

Now I would like to ask some of these people, would they be content with such a life? Would it be heaven to them, apart from all dearest to their nature? No, heaven extends through unlimited space, and is not confined to one particular spot. Think of the rapture of wandering from one glorious spot to another. And then, those who have the desire may hover near the loved ones left on earth.

Oh happy state! what joy it is to mingle, unseen, among the different worlds of God's creation! Many of them are much more beautiful than the earth you dwell on.

Do not wonder that the inhabitants of Brighter Spheres are so rarely visible to those on earth. It takes a strong power to enable us to materialize. Yet this power is valuable, for it would prove to unbelievers the truth of immortality.

As I hover near, dictating this, there softly comes to me the spirit of a woman, fair to look upon. I have met her before amid the glories of Brighter Spheres, where she unfolded to me a portion of her history. She had once stood visibly on earth. The way she relates the tale is as follows:—

Not long ago there dwelt beside the seashore a humble fisherman who was an Atheist; yet his only child—a daughter—was a sincere Christian. It was the only trial of her life, trying to convince her father of the truth.

One summer's day there came to that spot a youth—a descendant of a noble race. There, where the wild waves whispered to him of a brilliant future, he met his fate. He beheld the fair maiden, and it was the old story—a father's anger and a maiden's tears. The result was a quiet marriage; and forth from her home, into the world, she went. But soon came the awakening. Like some flower, transplanted from its native soil, she drooped, until at last death released her spirit; and her first thought was to try and let her father know that, though dead to the world he lived on, she still existed in a purer, better life.

It was night in the old man's dwelling, and for miles around the snow-drifts lay in an unbroken tract. The old home was inaccessible to the approach of man, but in the house an old neighbor was passing the night. He possessed the power of a medium. This drew the spirit of the maiden onward, till gradually she assumed the outward covering of the soul. She stood there, visible to the eyes of her father, and assured him of a future life; and then, as he tried to clasp her, she slowly vanished from his sight. Now he no longer doubts; he has seen proof of immortal life. I merely relate this because *that man is living yet*, and, if he reads this, can verify the statement.

And now one more scene before I close this record. It is my father's house, and he is alone. There is no joy around him, no mirth, no childish laughter. Bereft of earthly hope, for him the future holds nothing but despair. Sadness comes over my spirit as I behold him. Fain would I stand before him and tell him of my life, but the power is not there. Will he read this book, I wonder? If he does, my task will not have been in vain.

O God! who lovest all mankind, Thou knowest well my mission; in no other way but this could I accomplish it. Look Thou kindly upon it, O God! and send it forth into the doubting world with Thy earnest blessing.

And now the prophetic instinct steals upon my soul. I see mankind believing in this work. I see the world better, purer, for having read it. I see the bonds of brotherhood and love extending throughout the universe, and all voices acknowledging Christ as God.

And now farewell, O earth; nothing more remains to tell you, O people of the world! In a little while, perhaps, you will behold the glories I now revel in. Soon I shall ascend into a higher sphere, where new joys await me. Yet I will not desert you. When you see the trees budding forth in spring-time, I will have more to tell you. To those who will find fault with this work, I have but one excuse to offer. During life I was not a writer; and if I have accomplished in death what was not permitted in life, surely you can be lenient with all mistakes.

Now again I say, "farewell," with many thanks, to those who took an active part and deep interest in the production of this work —especially to her who, through many trials, never failed me yet. And when for each of you the Stream of Life is ended, and you stand upon the eternal shore, then shall I seek you, and we will wander together through the ever-increasing glory and delight of Brighter Spheres. Even now there comes to me the far-off echo of heavenly music. You cannot hear it, nor can you see the bright-robed messengers of mercy, who come to bear me upward. Shall I see the Saviour there, I wonder? Will He bless me for the task I have done? A flood of deep radiance steals over my soul; joy, rapture, glory, uplift me. Earth is fading from my sight. My mission is ended; my task is done. Brighter grows the light around me. I breathe on thee a blessing ere I vanish. Ah! I hear the Saviour calling on me from afar. To Thee, O Christ, my Lord, I come.

THE END.

www.ingramcontent.com/pod-product-compliance
Lightning Source LLC
Chambersburg PA
CBHW021832230426
43669CB00008B/944